D1241735

Theology of the Land

261.85
W3735

49436

Crossroads College
G.H. Cachiaras Memorial Library
920 Mayowood Road SW, Rochester MN 55902
507-535-3331

DEMCO

THEOLOGY
OF THE
LAND

Leonard Weber
Walter Bruggemann
C. Dean Freudenberger
John Hart
Richard Cartwright Austin

Bernard F. Evans
Gregory D. Cusack
Editors

THE LITURGICAL PRESS
Collegeville, Minnesota

Cover design by Joshua Jeide, O.S.B.

Copyright © 1987 by The Order of St. Benedict, Inc., Collegeville, Minnesota. All rights reserved. No part of this book may be reproduced in any form or by any means without written permission except in the case of brief quotations embodied in critical articles and reviews. For information address: The Liturgical Press, Collegeville, Minnesota 56321.

Manufactured in the United States of America.

1	2	3	4	5	6	7	8

Library of Congress Cataloging-in-Publication Data

Theology of the land.

Papers presented at the First Theology of Land Conference held at St. John's University in 1985.

1. Land tenure—Religious aspects—Christianity— Congresses.   I. Weber, Leonard J., 1942– II. Evans, Bernard F., 1943–   .   III. Cusack, Gregory D.   IV. Theology of Land Conference (1st : 1985 : St. John's University (Collegeville, Minn.))
BR115.L23T48   1987   261.8'5   87-4230
ISBN 0-8146-1554-6

Contents

The Contributors

LEONARD J. WEBER is the director of The Ethics Institute at Mercy College in Detroit.

WALTER BRUEGGEMANN is a professor at Columbia Theological Seminary in Decatur, Georgia.

C. DEAN FREUDENBERGER is professor of international development studies, missions, and the rural church at the school of theology, University of Claremont.

JOHN HART is associate professor of theology at Carroll College.

RICHARD CARTWIGHT AUSTIN is a minister with the Holston Presbytery of The Presbyterian Church.

BERNARD F. EVANS holds the Virgil Michel Ecumenical Chair in Rural Social Ministries at St. John's University in Minnesota.

GREGORY D. CUSACK is a former executive director of the National Catholic Rural Life Conference.

Introduction

In the past two decades our generation witnessed massive famines in Africa and other parts of the world. Ethiopia is one dramatic scene of the starvation and suffering that accompany a land's inability to yield food for its inhabitants. Unending series of draughts in countries plagued by war and social and political turmoil are readily cited as the cause of these famines. Yet many agronomists and agricultural scientists note that these tragedies were long in the making—that decades and centuries of farming techniques unsuitable for these soils prepared the way for extended draughts to have their most devastating impact on the land and its people.

Less visible than the famine of Ethiopia but no less destructive of human life is the chronic hunger that plagues millions of human beings. The 1981 Presidential Commission on World Hunger estimated that as many as 800 million people suffer from hunger. In some of the poorest nations this hunger co-exists with land use policies that divert land away from the production of food for local consumption.

Here in the United States thousands of moderate sized family farms close down each year—victims of social, economic, and political forces at work over the past forty years. As these farms are forced to shut down, their land is concentrated into a smaller and smaller number of cropland owners. This growing concentration of land ownership appears to have a negative impact on the economic and social well-being of our small towns and rural communities.

At the same time we see an increasing deterioration of our farmland soil and water supplies needed for agricultural production. In the United States and throughout the world soil erosion is at an all-time high. Both the smaller traditional family farms as well as the larger corporate farming enterprises exhibit the signs of cropland deterioration—the signs of the harm that is brought to our land through farming practices guided by profit more than stewardship.

These experiences of food shortages, deterioration of our farmland, and concentration in land ownership suggest a need for rethinking our relationship to the land. All of us have a stake in what happens to the land. For most of us, our separation from the land may further distance us from concern about what is happening on our nation's food-producing land. Nevertheless, we and our children have an important stake in the fundamental questions: Who should own the land? and, How should the land be used?

With these concerns before us, the Virgil Michel Chair at St. John's University and the National Catholic Rural Life Conference in Des Moines are engaged in an effort to develop a new ethic of land ownership and land use—an ethic that is informed by biblical and theological perspectives as well as the experience of God's people today.

We believe there are serious moral questions emerging from the current trend in United States agriculture and land ownership patterns. How American farmland is used, and by whom, has significance for global food needs in an expanding world population and for the changing social context of our rural communities. We believe it is imperative that every effort be made to ensure that ownership and use of farmland reflect the realities of a hungry world and the values inherent in local agriculture and the dependent rural communities.

The Theology of Land Project represents a multi-year effort to articulate a new ethic of land ownership and land use appropriate for the United States. This project invites theologians across denominational lines to articulate biblical and theological perspectives that may lead to this ethic. It is our hope that the insights of theologians may interact with the experiences of local church leaders and the people who live and work upon the land. To that end the Virgil Michel Chair and the National Catholic Rural Life Conference have initiated a series of annual Theology of Land Conferences. This volume represents the theological perspectives offered in our first Theology of Land Conference (1985). The task of the speakers at this conference was to articulate general dimensions of a new theology or ethic of land ownership and land use. We are grateful for their contributions and for their permission to publish the presentations, thus making them available to a wider audience of persons concerned about land stewardship, agriculture, and rural life.

Leonard Weber examines the economic philosophy that has shaped American attitudes toward property in general; he proposes alternative models and directions for socially responsible land ownership and use. Walter Brueggemann explores the biblical covenantal relationship as a way for us to speak about land management. C. Dean Freudenberger addresses the implications of a new land ethic for the food and environmental crisis that has spread across the entire globe. John Hart offers the creation-focused spirituality and religious faith of Native American peoples as a source for rethinking land ethics in America. Finally, Richard Austin proposes the rebuilding of human relationships with the land in the context of environmental concerns and the rights inherent in the land.

We are grateful to the Otto Bremer Foundation in St. Paul and to the Catholic Extension Society in Chicago for their financial support of the Theology of Land Conference and this publication.

Bernard F. Evans

1

Land Use Ethics: The Social Responsibility of Ownership

Leonard Weber

The manner in which I approach the question of land use ethics is influenced by my overall agenda as an ethicist. Four aspects of that agenda should be highlighted. First, I am committed to looking for connections between rural issues and urban issues. I am a resident of the city of Detroit. My roots are rural, and I continue to be vitally interested in rural issues, but I am now an urban man working at an urban institution. I am not comfortable when I hear advocates of rural justice talking about how our country is biased in favor of an urban ethic. [1] While there is much truth to the assertion that many of our leaders know next to nothing about rural life and about agriculture, I am not so sure that there is anything to be gained by talking about an urban ethic taking priority over a rural ethic. Rather, a more fruitful approach is to focus on some of the ethical beliefs that we have inherited and that may be contributing to the problems faced by both the rural disadvantaged and the urban disadvantaged.

Given this first item on my own agenda, my attention is directed not toward agriculture specifically—the use of cropland or rangeland—but toward the larger economic philosophy that has shaped American attitudes toward property generally. Land use has been greatly influenced by this philosophy, the same philosophy that has had tremendous implications for the ways we react to the poor in this country, whether they be urban poor or rural poor. One need not be an expert on rural issues to understand how this economic philosophy has influenced our attitudes toward land use. Nor need we be economists to appreciate the impact of that same economic philosophy upon the lives of low-income people everywhere in our society. To discuss this dominant economic philosophy is to discuss an issue of equal importance to both rural Minnesotans and urban Detroit residents.

In the second item on my agenda, I will discuss the different ways of doing ethics in terms of different people that one is trying to reach and in terms of different actions that one would like those people to take. My focus is primarily on public policy rather than on individual behavior or on drawing out the implications of religious beliefs. I want to focus my ethical analysis on those beliefs that have important implications on the formulation of public policy in this country. Other approaches, other points of focus, are important, of course, but my primary concern is to try to bring ethical discussion to bear on issues in a way that may have an impact on public policy.

There are important consequences of this way of defining my agenda. In the first place, it means that my approach will be much less directly theological than that of some others. I want to be able to speak to ethical issues in a way that allows others who do not share my religious beliefs to find common ground. I do not agree with those theologians who want to address public policy issues using specifically Christian symbols.[2] This presentation does not make any appeal to Scripture for the foundation of land use ethics. Instead, I make use of concepts like human rights and the common good and social responsibility. This is by design; it is the result of the overall agenda that I have set for myself as an ethicist and as a citizen.

The third part of my larger agenda is to focus on the values that have historically shaped American beliefs and policies. I find it very interesting that many Americans seem to see no great difference between the principles presented in the draft of the bishops' pastoral letter on the United States economy and the values that have shaped the American system. I can only conclude that they do not understand what the bishops' committee is saying or that they do not understand the American tradition—or they do not understand either of them. My suspicion is that many contemporary Americans do not really understand the American ethical heritage, and they do not understand the extent to which the heritage has shaped our national policies. Ideas have consequences, and if we wish to understand the present reality and know how to try to bring about some change in the present, we need to study the social philosophy, the ethical beliefs, of our own American past.

The fact that I sense this need to emphasize dominant values in the American tradition—so that we know exactly what is shaping our public philosophy and how to respond to that—gives me a different emphasis from others. I read with interest and much admiration *The Spirit of the Earth* by John Hart. In talking about the American tradition, Hart stressed that aspect of the American heritage that he sees converging with his own Christian theology of the land. It is only very late in the book (unless I missed it earlier) that he clearly acknowledges that his vision is at odds with the dominant American tradition:

> A word of caution, however; to work for stewardship of the land is to risk being called a "communist" in our U. S. society, for when you base your actions on fundamental biblical principles and commands, you enter into conflict with the prevailing American atheist ideology . . . into which most Americans have been socialized . . . and the prevailing American economic structure that is based on and promotes that ideology and its consequences.[3]

There is nothing inappropriate in pointing (as Hart does) to the radicals in the American tradition—people like Thomas Paine and Henry George—whose thought can be used to support one's own beliefs. But it is first necessary to try to make more clear why it is, for most Americans, that this vision is radical and morally unacceptable. At least in my agenda, the effort to understand the mainline tradition claims high priority.

The last introductory point that I want to make is in regard to my analysis as part of the whole process of moral decision-making. It has been pointed out that Christian ethical reflection can start at different points.[4] We could start with analysis of particular situations in which decisions have to be made. (Should a certain piece of prime farmland be prohibited from being converted to other uses? Should specific farm tax policies be changed?) Or we could start with basic theological affirmations. (What does it mean to be a Christian? To whom does the earth, the land, belong?). Or we could start with ethical principles. (To what extent does someone have the right to own and use land as exclusively his or her own? How do we balance concern for future generations with the desire for a high standard of living now?). A full ethical discussion will ultimately include all three aspects, but one cannot do everything at once, and there must be a starting point.

My focus is usually on the level of ethical principles. As an ethicist, I usually do not say much about the ways specific issues should be resolved, and I usually do not focus much attention (at least explicitly) on the most fundamental philosophical or theological convictions. My focus tends to be on the middle level—trying to clarify ethical principles which will guide decision-making in specific situations and which reflect sound theological and philosophical affirmations about God, human life, and the natural world.

It is my task to discuss the understanding of land-use ethics that is presently found in this country. This gives me the opportunity to describe the dominant American tradition as well as to reflect on alternative systems of social ethics. At the end of the presentation I will suggest what appears to be a useful direction to take in developing a framework and a vocabulary for a more adequate land use ethic.

I. ETHICS OF LAND USE: A VARIETY OF APPROACHES

As we consider the contemporary understanding of ethical responsibility in regard to land use, it is important to recognize that there are a variety of ethical approaches and positions. If I had more time and more insight, I would like to fully explore four different approaches that are alive today in the United States, but I will be able to describe only two of these ethical systems in any detail. I will first identify the four and then make a few comments on the two that I am not going to be able to explain more fully.

I have a tendency to give a name to any systematic approach to an ethical issue that I am studying. But the first approach I would like to give more attention to someday is one that I cannot yet appropriately name, probably because I am not able to adequately describe it. I am referring to an understanding of how one should treat the land that I associate with my own recent ancestors—and probably many of yours. I sense that those people who emigrated from Europe to America in the last century or century and a half and who became farmers in this country had a distinct relationship with the land. It was not the Mother Earth concept of the Native Americans; it was not as dominated by economic considerations as that which has shaped most public policy in this country; it is much more pragmatic and anthropocentric than contemporary ecologists would advocate; it views land as something to be closely connected to and not simply as a source of income. Beyond these generalizations, I cannot go very far in describing an attitude and a sense of ethical responsibility that continues to exist among a significant number of people who are on the land in the United States today. Perhaps others who are closer to the owner-operated farm than I can describe more clearly this tradition that appears to be a coherent land use ethic. It is an ethical system that to the best of my knowledge has not been adequately summarized in contemporary ethical discussions.

The second system of ethics, one that I will describe in some detail, is the dominant American social philosophy; I will refer to it as the Traditional Ethic. I will describe it as a general system of social ethics, not as one that is specifically focused on land use. It is my belief that our general understanding of how society should be organized and what values are most fundamental has had a direct impact on land use decisions, just as it has had a direct impact on how we respond to poverty, on what we expect of government, and on a whole wide range of other issues and concerns. I will return to this Traditional Ethic.

A third ethical approach is another that I will discuss in some detail. I call it the Communitarian Ethic[5]. This ethic, too, needs to be described in terms of its general beliefs, not just its understanding of land use responsibility. It is an alternative vision that addresses the same general concerns found in the Traditional Ethic and may thus have the same possibility of influencing most policy decisions made in our society, including decisions in regard to land use.

The fourth ethical approach of significance to this study can be called the Ecological Ethic. It is one that I *am* able to describe, though I will not do so extensively. In this understanding of ethical responsibility, a key focus is on the land itself, on the relationship that we need to have to the environment that supports our life.

Aldo Leopold, one of the earliest proponents of the ecological ethic, described our whole ethical tradition as still in a stage of growth and development. He pointed out that at one time certain human beings (slaves) were considered as having no rights whatsoever; they were simply property that the owner could use in any way he or she saw fit (and not be considered as acting immorally). What is needed today, Leopold argued, is an extension of the understanding of ethics to include a sense of responsibility to respect and preserve something else that has long been considered *mere property—* the natural environment. "All ethics so far evolved rest upon a single premise: that the individual is a member of a community of interdependent parts. . . . The land ethic simply enlarges the boundaries of the community to include soils, waters, plants, and animals, or collectively: the land."[6]

The land is not just property; it is not just a commodity; it is not even just a resource. It is not just something to be used for human welfare. The land is something to be valued for its own sake.

Leopold gave expression to one principle of the ecological ethic when he wrote, "A thing is right when it tends to preserve the integrity, stability and beauty of the biotic community. It is wrong when it tends otherwise."[7] Human beings have an obligation to respect nature and preserve its integrity.

Sara Ebenreck has attempted to work out for agricultural ethics the implications of recognizing that the land has intrinsic value. She calls her approach "a partnership farmland ethic."[8]

Respect for land does not mean that land is not to be used. But it does mean that we should use land only in the same sense that it is appropriate to use persons. It is moral to use a person only in a way that is not destructive of that person and in a way that returns something of value to the one being used. Thus I use a secretary, and she uses my need for gainful employment.[9]

But to show proper respect for the land, it might be better to speak of "working with" rather than "using." "Because *working with* seems immediately to imply a partnership, a gradual shift of language so as to think of farming as 'working with' the land rather than 'using' it might in itself help to promote the ideas of respect for the land."[10]

A partnership land ethic implies, according to Ebenreck, three principles: "(1) respect for the fundamental nature of the land, (2) use that does not destroy that nature, and (3) returning something of value in exchange for the use."[11] Crops should be grown that are in harmony with the land's sustainable limits of soil, water, and nutrients. Knowing the land is essential for respect; this might mean that small-scale agriculture is more in harmony with respect for nature than large-scale agriculture.[12]

On the basis of my observation, it seems that the Ecological Ethic has not yet been widely accepted in this country and has not had much impact on public policies, economic decisions, or even on life-styles. This approach is worthy of much more attention, but may have to wait for another time (or for another writer).

The four ethical approaches that I have identified provide a good idea of the range of alternative approaches. One of these value systems—the Traditional Ethic—has been by far the most influential in this country. The other three are all at odds with the Traditional Ethic in significant ways and are possible alternatives if we are looking to develop a new dominant value system. At this point, it seems as though the Communitarian value system (or some variation thereof) has the greatest possibility of beginning to replace the Traditional Ethic. So I will turn to a discussion of those two.

II. The Traditional Ethic

During the last two hundred years and more, the system of social ethics that has dominated America and Americans is the set of beliefs that has found philosophical expression in the work of men like John Locke and Adam Smith. It is hard to think of anyone who has been more influential in shaping American social and political beliefs than these two thinkers. [13]

In this Traditional Ethic, the focus is primarily on individuals, who are seen as seeking their own economic self-interest. In this understanding of human nature, altruism (unselfish concern for the welfare of others) cannot really be expected to play any role in society. The best economic and political system is one that allows all of us to pursue our own interest as we ourselves define those interests. It is important that we recognize that this social value system is not really advocating selfishness in the sense that one doesn't really care what happens to others. Rather, what is involved here is the belief that the best way to contribute to the welfare of all is for each of us to concentrate on self. If I take care of my needs and you take care of your needs, then we will all benefit.

This is a social philosophy that expresses the belief that the best government is that which governs least—that the government is a threat to human freedoms and that "big government" is the biggest threat of all. Let me try to explain this antigovernment attitude in terms of the understanding of human rights found in this Traditional school of thought.

The Traditional understanding of human rights is that these rights are best thought of as individual freedoms. The human rights that are identified most frequently are the ones we associate with the Bill of Rights: freedom of speech and of the press, freedom from arbitrary arrest, freedom of religion. Usually included among the human rights is the opportunity to participate in the selection of political leaders. Of fundamental importance is the right to possess private property and, with few restrictions, to use that property as the owner sees fit.

In the Traditional view, human rights are asserted over against the government. While there may be other threats to human rights, the major threat is government itself. In order to protect the individual and his or her rights, it is necessary to restrict the power and the role of the government.

In this system of social ethics, government has only one legitimate purpose—the protection of the rights of individuals. This is the reason why governments are instituted in the lives of human beings. The government is appropriately involved in providing for national defense and in protecting individuals from criminals. The government's proper role, therefore, is a negative one—to protect against threats and against evildoers. It is not the government's responsibility to attempt to assert a more positive function, the function of assuring that human needs are being met. That is the role of individuals (and of families and of voluntary associations); for the government to be involved in trying to assure that everyone's human needs are met would mean government interference with what are private and personal responsibilities. When the government is seeking to positively promote human welfare, it is inclining in the direction of denying human freedoms.

As indicated earlier, the right to own and use private property is at the heart of this Traditional social value system. Every system of social ethics includes a model of distributive justice, an understanding of the best and most fair way of distributing the benefits and burdens of society among the members of that society. As you would no doubt expect, the model of distributive justice that goes hand in hand with the value system that I have been discussing is a model that allows for no significant role for the government. If we are seeking the most just society, the wealth of that society should be distributed according to a method that respects individual rights and individual claims to private property. The best method—and according to the proponents of this view, the only just method—of determining who gets what is through a system of private exchange of goods and services. This is the system that we have come to call capitalism or the free enterprise system or the market system. The market system does not guarantee that everyone's material needs will be met; it is not a system that is primarily designed to ensure that everyone's material needs are met. The system is primarily designed to allow for whatever will happen when individuals freely pursue their own paths.

Ever since Adam Smith, proponents of the market system have argued that it not only keeps government "off our backs" but that it also produces greater wealth than any other system. I do not intend to go into that aspect of the social value system very extensively; I simply want to note that it includes the belief that the very best way to respond to poverty is to allow the free market system to function without interference because the result will be greater productivity; and productivity, more than anything else, will help the poor rise out of poverty.

One last general comment about the Traditional Ethic—a comment about taxation. It follows clearly from everything that has already been said about this social value system that taxation is very hard to accept. Taxation involves the taking of private property from individuals to support government programs. The only justification for taxes is the need to protect against threats to persons and property. Taxation that is directed to spending for social programs is basically unacceptable because it amounts to a redistribution of income, the taking of the property of some to give to others; it is akin to robbery. According to the Traditional value system, the wealth of society is to be distributed through the market system, not through government programs.

A few examples of ways in which this traditional American ethic has been expressed may be useful in recognizing the pervasiveness of this philosophy and the impact that this value system has had on the ways in which Americans view their social obligations.

The first example that I want to use is Andrew Carnegie. Carnegie was the poor immigrant boy who became one of the richest men in America. In 1889 he published an essay on what men of wealth should do with that wealth. Carnegie's "Gospel of Wealth" was an effort to explain the moral responsibility of those who, like himself, have become very wealthy in a society in which not everyone can be successful. A few excerpts will give something of the flavor of the Carnegie Gospel.

> Today the world obtains commodities of excellent quality at prices which even the generation preceding this would have deemed incredible. In the commercial world similar causes have produced similar results, and the race is benefited thereby. The poor enjoy what the rich could not before afford. What were the luxuries have become the necessities of life. The laborer has now more comforts than the farmer had a few generations ago. The farmer has more luxuries than the landlord had, and is more richly clad and better housed. . . .

> The price we pay for this salutary change is, no doubt, great. We assemble thousands of operatives in the factory, in the mine, and in the counting-houses of whom the employer can know little or nothing, and to whom the employer is little better than a myth. All intercourse between them is at an end. Rigid castes are formed, and, as usual, mutual ignorance breeds mutual distrust. Each caste is without sympathy for the other, and ready to credit anything disparaging in regard to it. Under the law of competition, the employer of thousands is forced into strictest economics, among which the rates paid to labor figure prominently, and often there is friction between the employer and the employed, between capital and labor, between rich and poor. Human society loses homogeneity.

The price which society pays for the law of competition, like the price it pays for cheap comforts and luxuries, is also great but the advantages of this law are also greater still, for it is to this law that we owe our wonderful material development, which brings improved conditions in its train . . . .

It is a law, as certain as any of the others named, that men possessed of this peculiar talent for affairs, under the free play of economic forces, must, of necessity, soon be in receipt of more revenue than can be judiciously expended upon themselves; and this law is as beneficial for the race as the others . . . .

This, then, is held to be the duty of the man of Wealth: First, to set an example of modest, unostentatious living, shunning display or extravagance, to provide moderately for the legitimate wants of those dependent upon him, and after doing so to consider all surplus revenues which come to him simply as trust funds, which he is called upon to administer, and strictly bound as a matter of duty to administer in the manner which, in his judgement, is best calculated to produce the most beneficial results for the community—the man of wealth thus becoming the mere agent and trustee for his poorer brethren, bringing to their service his superior wisdom, experience, and ability to administer, doing for them better than they would or could do for themselves.

. . . Those who would administer wisely must, indeed, be wise, for one of the serious obstacles to the improvement of our race is indiscriminate charity. It were better for mankind that the millions of the rich were thrown into the sea than so spent as to encourage the slothful, the drunken, the unworthy. Of every thousand dollars spent in so-called charity today, it is probable that $950 is unwisely spent: so spent, indeed, as to produce the very evils which it proposes to mitigate or cure . . . .

In bestowing charity, the main consideration should be to help those who will help themselves; to provide part of the means by which those who desire to improve may do so; to give those who desire to rise the aids by which they may rise; to assist, but rarely or never to do all. Neither the individual nor the race is improved by almsgiving. Those worthy of assistance, except in rare cases, seldom require assistance. The really valuable men of the race never do, except in cases of accident or sudden change . . . .

Thus is the problem of Rich and Poor to be solved. The laws of accumulation will be left free; the laws of distribution free. Individualism will continue, but the millionaire will be but a trustee for the poor; intrusted for a season with a great part of the increased wealth of the community, but administering it for the community far better than it could or would have done for itself . . . .[14]

There are clearly two major components in Carnegie's Gospel: (1) that the system of private pursuit of economic self-interest is good (and it is good because it increases productivity and thereby raises the standard of living for everyone); and (2) that practices and policies should be such that they do not reward vice and laziness (the very fact that some are poor is a sign of their being undeserving).

A second expression of the Traditional Ethic and a much more contemporary one, is a Mobil Corporation advertisement from a few years ago. The advertisement is in the form of an editorial commentary and seems to be in response to those who argue that the American system of high-level consumption is ethically questionable.

Judging by some of what we read and hear, self-flagellation seems about to become the order of the day. Much of whatever Americans do or achieve or enjoy is termed immoral or otherwise indefensible, and what people in other countries do is hailed as the shape of the future, morally speaking.

Well now.

A lot of this national guilt complex depends on how things are put.

Suppose, for example, we ask you, "Do you think it's right for the United States, with only 4% of the world's population, to consume 26% of its energy?" That might be your cue to beat your breast and cry, "Heavens to Betsy, no! How could we do such a thing? And how can we atone?"

Suppose, however, we rephrase that question and ask you, "Isn't it remarkable that the United States, with only a twentieth of the world's population, can produce a fourth of the entire world's goods and services? And that we have become the industrial and agricultural breadbasket of the world . . . . a prime purveyor to the hungry and the needy abroad?"

"Gee," you might say, "Just shows you what the old Yankee ingenuity, along with hard work and clean living, can do."

We can stomach breast-beating or a hairshirt demonstration, if that's what gives the other fellow his kicks. But the point we want to make is that nobody in this country has to beat himself over the head just because he's adequately fed and clothed. Mankind has always striven for a land flowing with milk and honey, long on deprivation and longer on austerity . . . .

The point is that our country is so productive, despite all the roadblocks thrown up by the government and others, that it can turn out an almost unbelievable volume of goods—enough to supply the domestic market and still have a lot left over to export. If you want more U.S. money and food and other goods sent to needy peoples abroad, fine; tell your Senators and your Congressman so. But don't feel guilty about living well if you already do, or about wanting to if you don't.

We are not trying to promote gluttony or even conspicuous consumption. We *are* trying to deflate what strikes us as nonsense. Life is short, and people who work hard and productively shouldn't reproach themselves over their rewards, especially since producing for plenty makes society a lot more comfortable than sharing unnecessary shortage . . . .[15]

Mobil's Gospel is not very different from Carnegie's Gospel: the system is good because it is productive, and those who are successful should feel that they have deserved it— not that they are depriving others of necessities.

My third example of the Traditional American Social Ethic is Milton Friedman. Economist Friedman is a leading opponent of the belief that businesses have a social responsibility, a moral responsibility that goes beyond their seeking profit. (I will return to the concept of social responsibility a little later.) Friedman has written:

Few trends could so thoroughly undermine the very foundation of our free society as the acceptance by corporate officials of a social responsibility other than to make as much money for their stock holders as possible. This is a fundamentally subversive doctrine. [16]

The doctrine of the social responsibility of business is subversive for Friedman because it requires that attention be given to what is for the public good rather than to what is for the private good. For Friedman, it means that we are moving in a direction in which, at some point, it will become acceptable for someone outside of business to tell those *in* business what their responsibility is, what is best for society. To put it differently, someone else will tell individuals what to do with their property. This is fundamentally subversive to someone like Friedman because it suggests public control over private property and thereby threatens basic freedoms.

The right to own private property (like land) and the right to use that property as the owner sees fit is part of a larger social philosophy that is deeply ingrained in the American mentality. The perception of land as a resource to be used primarily for private profit is a natural corollary of this philosophy. A discussion of land use ethics of the sort that is being undertaken with this Theology of the Land Project should recognize that land use questions must be seen in the context of a whole system of social ethics.

The land use ethic that contemporary American society has inherited is primarily an economic ethic. The value of land is determined almost completely by its role in the market system. Land, like any other resource, is worth only what you can get for it. It is worth what you can do with it or perhaps to it; its value is what you can sell it or its products for. [17] In this ethical system, land has value precisely as property. Land is not considered good in and of itself; it is good only if it is good for something. Its value is instrumental, not intrinsic.

In Traditional thought, land has no real value until it is "improved." In John Locke's labor theory of value, land acquires its value when labor is mixed with it. When land is not "improved" through labor, it remains waste and is without any real value. When the farmer works the land, "the results are *improvements,* a key term in homesteading days and even today in rural America . . ."[18]

While not everyone today fully accepts the position that has been the dominant one historically in this country, the strength of that tradition is still very great. The tendency to think of land as an economic resource to be used primarily for private profit is part of a system of belief that ties together three extremely important convictions: that the traditional system of individualism and profit-seeking best (1) contributes to productivity; (2) protects individual human rights from violation by government; (3) rewards those who deserve rewards.

III. The Communitarian Ethic

While the Communitarian Ethic has not yet had a major impact on the development of American institutions and policies, it is a philosophy that is not unfamiliar on the American scene. It is reflected to a significant degree in the draft of the Catholic bishops' pastoral letter on the United States economy.

The starting point of the Communitarian value system is the belief that men and women are, by their very nature, social beings. They are not isolated individuals who choose to come together in society only because it is necessary to do so to protect their individual rights and their individual freedoms; rather, individuals and human rights always need to be understood in a social context. Fundamental to the moral responsibility of every individual is the obligation to contribute to the common good. The good of the whole human family is the goal, because individuals find their own meaning and identity as part of that human family.

At the time of the French Revolution, the three goals of the new society were liberty, equality, and fraternity. In American intellectual history, liberty has been highlighted and, as I have indicated, liberty remains the key goal in the Traditional value system. Some attention has been paid to equality historically, but the ideal of fraternity has gotten very little recognition. Fraternity (or community, to use a nonsexist term) involves cooperation, solidarity, and commitment to common goals. The Communitarian value system is a set of beliefs that attempts to evaluate the concept of community to the level of freedom and equality in our social goals and ideals.

While the Traditional view is very uneasy with the concept of social responsibility in economic endeavors, the Communitarian view is very much at home with that concept. Social responsibility clearly identifies the obligation to be aware of and concerned about the impact of one's actions on others in society. None of us lives in a vacuum; we should be constantly trying to promote those activities that have the most beneficial impact on the lives of others. This orientation, rather than the pursuit of economic self-interest, should guide behavior.

Just as in the Traditional system of social ethics, human rights occupy an important position in the Communitarian view. But the human rights insisted upon here are expanded to include economic/social human rights as well as civil/political human rights. The civil/political human rights are the ones that I identified in describing the Traditional view—the various freedoms that individuals can claim over against government. The economic/social human rights are quite different; these are the claims that individuals can make to the basic necessities of life. If we acknowledge that there are economic human rights, then we are saying that all individuals, regardless of their ability to provide for themselves, have a legitimate claim—have a right—to such things as food, clothing, shelter, employment, and health care. If these are human rights, then all of society has the obligation to see that these basic human requirements are met for everyone. As the Roman Catholic bishops express themselves in their pastoral letter on *Catholic Social Teaching and the U.S. Economy*, the work of ensuring that everyone's essential needs are met must begin with

> the development of a new cultural concensus that the basic economic conditions of human welfare are essential to human dignity and are due persons by right (no. 83).

If society has the obligation to ensure that everyone has the essentials of a life with dignity, then the economic and political institutions of society must be structured in such a way that people do have enough to eat and do have employment. In the Communitarian view, much more is involved than being compassionate or humanitarian toward those in need. While it may be necessary to have programs designed to provide direct support for those in need, the more fundamental commitment should be to develop a system that ensures, as much as possible, that poverty and hunger do not happen. Society has an obligation—and it is hard to see how this can happen without a major role for government—to see to it that economic and political structures are based on respect for economic human rights.

From the perspective of the Communitarian Ethic, the government is not looked upon as the enemy (or potential enemy) of the people. The government is looked upon as one very important part of the mechanism necessary to give guidance and direction to economic behavior and to the distribution of wealth. Society has the responsibility to see to it that wise stewardship is exercised over the limited available resources. The government has a key role to play in planning and overseeing.

As I understand the various positions on individual rights, on the role of the government, and on social responsibility, one of the most significant positions within the Communitarian view is its position on the right to private property. Private ownership has to be subordinated to common use. The resources of the earth exist for the benefit of all. Private ownership may be an appropriate way of administering those resources for the most part, but private ownership means stewardship or trusteeship, not the right to do whatever one wants. No one has a right to claim for his or her exclusive use more than is needed when others do not have enough to meet their essential needs.

The concept of property rights goes hand in hand with the concept of distributive justice in the Communitarian Ethic. Because the wealth and benefits of society belong, ultimately, to everyone, that wealth should not be distributed unrestrictedly by the market system. The market system, after all, allows some to make millions a year while others have no market value at all—it simply depends upon how fortunate one is in providing goods or services that others are willing to pay for. A just society is one in which the wealth is distributed in such a way that everyone's essential needs are met. This is not to be interpreted that everyone is to be exactly equal economically. It simply means that there is a minimum level under which no one should be allowed to fall. Nothing else is compatible with the basic Communitarian belief that the resources exist for the common good.

In his important study of the Catholic human rights tradition, David Hollenbach articulates three priority principles of justice:

1. The needs of the poor take priority over the wants of the rich.

2. The freedom of the dominated takes priority over the liberty of the powerful.

3. The participation of marginalized groups takes priority over the preservation of an order which excludes them.[19]

What Hollenbach's priority principles do is put the emphasis on the poor and the disadvantaged. Meeting their needs comes first, in terms of moral claims and moral obligations. This is, of course, entirely at odds with the Traditional American Ethic—the success ethic that has seen poverty as an indication of laziness or moral turpitude. The difference is a reflection of the different starting points. The Traditional Ethic starts with the emphasis on individual freedom, while the Communitarian Ethic starts with an emphasis on the common good. As a result, each ethic reaches different conclusions in regard to the poor and the disadvantaged.

Some may think it a little strange that in the Communitarian view, with its commitment to the common good, the particular focus is often on only those in society who are poor or disadvantaged in some way. But putting the needs of the disadvantaged first is not, in any way, in contradiction to the commitment to the common good. Since the common good is defined, in part, by meeting the essential needs of all, the effort to promote the common good requires focusing on those whose needs are not now being adequately addressed.

The type of land use ethic that follows from the basic premises of the Communitarian Ethic is not difficult to see. The understanding of who should control the land and for what purposes would be very different from the Traditional approach. Albert Fritsch has written on land use from, I think, largely a Communitarian perspective.

> People have a right to land, but this is a communal rather than an individual right. The local community has a right to access to its land, and to be empowered to distribute that land in such manner that the health and welfare of the community is best served. Corporate or "legal" persons do not enjoy a right to land as such, but exist at the pleasure of the people. When corporate lands are found to be excessive from the standpoint of community well-being, a redistribution program should be exacted. Small family holdings should be encouraged as better suited to land stewardship and conservation . . . .

> Land use planning is a necessity for the integrity of the community. It must include citizen participation and decision-making and be as decentralized in nature and structure as the local conditions allow . . . .

> While those who disturb land must be made to restore it to its original condition, it is the local community's responsibility to oversee the operation and to judge ultimate use of the land. [20]

Let me turn now to my own suggestions about one road we might take from here in developing an adequate land use ethic for this country today.

IV. PROPERTY RIGHTS AND SOCIAL RESPONSIBILITY

What I am calling the Communitarian value system may not be as fully developed as it will need to be in order to be completely satisfactory. There is, it seems to me, some lack of clarity regarding the relationship between negative human rights and positive human rights. Which should claim higher priority: freedom from governmental interference in the private lives of individuals or assurance that everyone's essential economic needs are met? The Traditional American Ethic clearly puts negative human rights first; the Communitarian Ethic insists that positive human rights are also of fundamental importance, but it is not clear, at least to me, how to work out the relationship between the positive and the negative. How much freedom should be sacrificed to meet essential needs (if, in fact, setting up that sort of opposition is even legitimate)?

As we continue to develop our understanding of human rights, we need to answer the question of what are essential rights, basic claims that must be satisfied before someone can be said to be living a minimally dignified human life. As John Coleman argues, we need a theory of basic rights—and we need to develop such a theory for two reasons: "First, such a theory seems necessary to adjudicate, with any rigor, conflicting claims to rights. Second, it provides us with a priority list of rights to press in human rights advocacy."[21] If we do not develop an understanding of what rights are really basic and really essential, then it becomes very difficult to respond adequately to all sorts of claims of "rights."

I have often expressed hesitation over the "rights" approach to resolving moral dilemmas (or developing public policy). To argue for the "right" to do this or the "right" to do that may often lead persons to focus on what they can get for themselves; it is in many ways an expression of an individualistic ethic. To approach moral questions from the point of view of basic human rights is, though, a little different. The focus here is not so much on what I can claim for myself, but on what is essential to human dignity and what everyone, therefore, must have. To talk about human rights is to talk more about the claims made upon us than it is to talk about getting what we can for ourselves. It is to think more about our social obligations than it is to think about what we have coming.

So I want to turn from this discussion of human rights to a discussion of property rights—and I want to do that in the context of social obligation or social responsibility. Given our economic orientation and given our ethical heritage, a focus on land ownership may be the best way into a practically useful ethic of land use.

I would like to make use of the concept of social responsibility in an attempt to delineate some ethical principles or guidelines in regard to ownership of land. The traditional emphasis has been on ownership rights, on property rights. A human rights starting point that recognizes social/economic rights as well as civil/political rights leads us to talk about responsibility toward others. The concept of social responsibility has become a widely used term to discuss moral obligations in business. I am suggesting that we borrow this term and concept from business ethics and begin to use it in our attempts to understand and articulate moral obligation in land use.

Milton Friedman to the contrary, there is a quite widely accepted belief today that businesses do have social responsibility and that this responsibility goes beyond responsibility to the stockholders. (One major study of readers of the *Harvard Business Review* found that 69 percent agreed to the statement that "profit is really a somewhat ineffective measure of business's social effectiveness.")[22]

When people are asked what the purpose of business is, many do immediately respond by saying that the purpose of business is to make a profit. But that is only a part of what people believe about business. Most of us, if we take the time to think about it, would acknowledge that there are many things that we would not do, even though they are profitable. We might find a statement by Kenneth Mason very appropriate. Mason, a former president of Quaker Oats, said: "Making a profit is no more the purpose of a corporation than getting enough to eat is the purpose of life."[23] The purpose of business is to provide needed goods and service; making a reasonable profit makes it possible for one to continue to provide those goods and services and at the same time to make a decent living for oneself and for one's dependents.

Institutions that engage in economic activity often have an immense impact upon society, upon the quality of life of many people. They cannot simply be looked upon as "private" enterprises, and this reality is becoming recognized more and more.

A useful starting point for considering the basis for the concept of social responsibility is in terms of the "social contract upon which basis the corporation functions."[24] Society grants the corporation its rights. "By issuing a corporate charter, it endows the corporation with certain legal privileges (including a franchise to do business, the privilege of limited liability as an aid to assembling capital, and the right to sue and to be sued as an individual citizen). . . ."[25] In return, society expects certain types of corporate behavior.

The terms of the past social contract were quite clear. Since economic growth was viewed as necessary for all progress, business was expected and encouraged to pursue growth. Because technological advance was thought to fuel economic growth, technology was an unquestioned good. Because "the engine of economic growth was identified as the drive for profits by unfettered, competitive, private enterprise,"[26] business was to be free from constraints. The beliefs on which the past contract was based have been greatly weakened. Many now think that further economic growth is frequently destructive, that some new technologies are dehumanizing, and, especially, that unfettered business is contrary to the common good. A new social contract is gradually emerging, one that includes quite different expectations of business from the past.

The relationship between profit-making and social responsibility in a private profit system needs reconsideration. A typical position taken by business persons is that socially responsible actions can be supported that reduce short-range profits if they are likely to improve long-range profits, that business "will not take actions which will reduce both short-range and long-range profits."[27] I do not think this position is adequate. The social contract with business should no longer be based on the belief that the first responsibility of business is to make a profit. What should be expected of business is that it be beneficial to society. Daniel Lufkin has called for a redefinition of the concept of profit, "one that will assess corporate gains and losses, not only in terms of dollars but also in terms of social benefits realized."[28] If this definition of profit were accepted, profit might be precisely what society demands of business: but this, however, is clearly not the usual understanding of the term. If there is a conflict between profit and social benefit, social benefit must come first. The social contract should not provide business with the right to do injury. Business exists to benefit society; where it is not doing that, it cannot even argue the right to exist.

On the basis of the comments that I have made about basic human rights and about social responsibility, I turn now to ethical reflections in regard to property ownership, one of the key considerations in land use ethics.

The right to private ownership (for example, of the land) should not be thought of as a basic human right. As Patricia Werhane points out, it is not on a par with basic rights, "because one could live fully as a human being and develop freely as a person without the right to private ownership . . . ."[29] I do not want to suggest that private ownership is inappropriate; I do want to argue that private ownership with the claim to the right to do whatever one wants with the property is inappropriate. Just as there is a social responsibility to business, so there is a social responsibility to ownership (especially ownership of productive property). I agree with the Communitarian emphasis on the common good orientation of property. The American Catholic bishops, in an early draft of their economics pastoral, make the point very clearly that, reviewing Church history, "We find a constant affirmation that the goods of this earth are common property and that men and women are summoned to faithful stewardship rather than to selfish appropriation or exploitation of what is destined for all."[30] One of the clearest expressions of this conviction is found in *Populorum Progressio* by Pope Paul VI: "Private property does not constitute for anyone an absolute unconditioned right. No one is justified in keeping for his exclusive use what he does not need, when others lack necessities."[31] Land ownership involves significant social responsibility.

William Everett has identified four specific ownership rights: the right of use, the right of income, the right of transfer, the right of alteration.[32] *Use* means occupancy or exploitation (in a neutral sense of the term). It involves the use of the land in a way that does not alter its continuing use. *Income* refers to the fruits of the property. The right of *transfer* means the right to sell the land, give it away, or leave it as a legacy. *Alteration* of land includes mineral extraction, industrial activity, construction, depositing of wastes, removal or addition of certain components to the land (erosion?). Alterations means those changes that involve the long-range destruction of certain land uses.[33]

The right of development is the same as Everett's right of alteration. Of the four rights involved in land ownership, this one is the least defensible as a private right. Social responsibility requires that we recognize that development rights are limited by human needs and the needs of the environment. The destruction of the possibility of certain land uses, such as cropland, is to be considered just and moral only if it does not reduce the possibility of meeting these needs. *One way, perhaps the only effective way, of recognizing that individuals do not have the right to do what they please with the land is to deny that ownership includes development rights.* Development may sometimes be justifiable, but it is not the individual's "right" to develop the land as he or she sees fit.

What I am suggesting is that we might want to make use of the evolving concept of social responsibility (within a framework of an emphasis on basic human rights) and that we might want to use it in a way that begins to bring elements of a new social value system right into the heart of contemporary discussion of economic policy and land use policy. The concept might allow us to move away from the emphasis on individual rights toward an emphasis on the common good without having to invent a whole new ethical vocabulary for the American public.

1. Victor Ray, "Survival and the Urban Ethic," *Catholic Rural Life*, 35 (July, 1985), pp. 17–18.

2. See Richard John Neuhaus, *The Naked Public Square* (Grand Rapids, Mich.: William B. Eerdmans, 1984) for an example of the argument that the public philosophy must be religiously based. See also my review of Neuhaus' book in *Horizons*, 12 (Spring 1985), pp. 212–13.

3. John Hart, *The Spirit of the Earth* (New York: Paulist Press, 1984), p. 148.

4. See Merle Longwood, "The Common Good: An Ethical Framework for Evaluating Environmental Issues," *Theological Studies*, 34 (September, 1973), p. 469.

5. The term "Communitarian" has been taken from "Social Value Systems Analysis" published by the Center for Ethics and Social Policy (Berkeley, Calif.) in 1978. The explanation of what this ethical system involves is largely my own.

6. Aldo Leopold, "The Land Ethic," in Paul Shepard and Daniel McKinley (eds.), *The Subversive Science: Essays Toward an Ecology of Man*, (Boston: Houghton Mifflin Col, 1969), p. 403.

7. Aldo Leopold, quoted in Peter Heinegg, "Ecology and Social Justice; Ethical Dilemmas and Revolutionary Hopes," *Environmental Ethics*, 1 (Winter 1979), p. 326.

8. Sara Ebenreck, "A Partnership Farmland Ethic," *Environmental Ethics*, 5 (Spring 1983), p. 36.

9. *Ibid.*, p. 41.

10. *Ibid.*, p. 42.

11. *Ibid.*

12. *Ibid.*, pp. 43–44.

13. Much of the general descriptions of "The Traditional Ethic" and of "The Communitarian Ethic" that follows is taken from a paper, "Meeting Human Needs: The Role of Government," that I presented at a conference on "Meeting Basic Needs in U.S. Society" in Detroit, April 1985.

14. Andrew Carnegie's essay, "Wealth," was first published in *The North American Review* in 1889. These selections are taken from the reprint of that essay found in George Bedell, Leo Sandon, and Charles Wellborn, *Religion in America* (New York: Macmillan, 1975), pp. 305–9.

15. The advertisement has the heading: "The national guilt complex. Achievement or original sin. Production vs. atonement." It is found in the July 8, 1978 issue of *The Saturday Review*.

16. Milton Friedman, "The Social Responsibility of Business," in Tom Beauchamp and Norman Bowie (eds.), *Ethical Theory and Business* (Englewood Cliffs, N.J.: Prentice-Hall, 1979), p. 136.

17. Mark Sagoff, "Do We Need a Land Use Ethic?" *Environmental Ethics*, 3 (Winter 1981), p. 297.

18. Eugene Hargrove, "Anglo-American Land Use Attitudes," *Environmental Ethics*, 2 (Summer 1980), p. 140.

19. David Hollenbach, *Claims in Conflict: Retrieving and Renewing the Catholic Human Rights Tradition* (New York: Paulist Press, 1979), p. 204.

20. Albert Fritsch, *Green Space: A Citizen's Guide to Proper Land Use* (Lexington, Ky.: Appalachia-Science in the Public Interest, 1982), pp. 155, 176, 188.

21. John Coleman, "Catholic Human Rights Theory: Four Challenges to an Intellectual Tradition." *The Journal Of Law and Religion*, 2 (1984), p. 355.

22. Steven Brenner and Earl Molander, "Is the Ethics of Business Changing?" in Thomas Donaldson and Patricia Werhane (eds.), *Ethical Issues in Business* (Englewood Cliffs, N.J.: Prentice Hall, 1979), p. 341.

23. Quoted in Robert Krikorian, "Plain Talk About the Public Trust," in Donald Jones (ed.), *Business, Religion, and Ethics* (Cambridge, Mass.: Oelgeschlager, Gunn & Hain, Publishers, 1982), p. 163.

24. John Corson and George Steiner, *Measuring Business's Social Performance: The Corporate Social Audit* (New York: Committee for Economic Development, 1974), p. 43.

25. *Ibid.*

26. Melvin Anshen, "Changing the Social Contract: A Role for Business," in Beauchamp and Bowie, *op. cit.*, p. 144.

27. George Steiner, *Business and Society* (New York: Random House, 1975), p. 159.

28. John Simon, Charles Powers, Jon Gunnemann, *The Ethical Investor* (New Haven: Yale University Press, 1972), p. 46.

29. Patricia Werhane, *Persons, Rights, & Corporations* (Englewood Cliffs, N.J.: Prentice-Hall, 1985), p. 21.

30. American Catholic bishops' pastoral letter, *Catholic Social Teaching and the U.S. Economy*, no. 33.

31. Pope Paul VI, *On the Development of Peoples* (Washington: United States Catholic Conference, 1967), no. 23.

32. William Everett, "Land Ethics: Toward a Covenantal Model," *1979 Selected Papers* (Newton Centre, Mass.: The American Society of Christian Ethics), pp. 51–54.

33. *Ibid.*

2

Land: Fertility and Justice

Walter Brueggemann

The Theology of Land project addresses the following questions:

    a) What is the operative land ethic in our society?

    b) What should be a sound theology of land?

    c) What does our connectedness to the land require?

Human connectedness to the land is suggested in biblical language by a play on words. *'Adam*, that is humankind, has as partner and mate, *'adamah* (land). [1] Humankind and land are thus linked in a covenantal relationship, analogous to the covenantal relationship between man and woman. [2] A sound theology requires honoring covenantal relationship. The operating land ethic in our society denies that relationship at enormous cost not only to land but to our common humanity.

I. WOMEN AND LAND

I begin with a most suggestive statement from Wendell Berry, who has reflected on land as much as anyone I know. He writes:

I do not know how exact a case might be made, but it seems to me that there is an historical parallel, in white American history, between the treatment of the land and the treatment of women. The frontier, for instance, was notoriously exploitative of both, and I believe for largely the same reasons. Many of the early farmers seem to have worn out farms and wives with equal regardlessness, interested in both mainly for what they would produce, crops and dollars, labor and sons; they clambered upon their fields and upon their wives, struggling for an economic foothold, the having and holding that cannot come until both fields and wives are properly cherished. And today there seems to me a distinct connection between our nomadism (our "social mobility") and the nearly universal disintegration of marriages and families. [3]

On the land theme, he comments:

The rural community—that is, the land and the people—is being degraded in complementary fashion by the specialists' tendency to regard the land as a factory and the people as spare parts. Or, to put it another way, the rural community is being degraded by the fashionable premise that the exclusive function of the farmer is production and that his major discipline is economics. [4]

The relation between women and land, between sexuality and economics, is the theme I want to pursue, to suggest that sexuality (which here includes fertility and production) and economics (which here includes the question of justice) cannot be separated. Sexuality and economics are the two great spheres of our life, the ones about which we most trouble, over which we most quarrel, and toward which we most hope. When sexuality is connected to fertility, and when economics is connected to justice, we are close to the core of all biblical ethics, for the Bible insists that fertility is impossible without justice; that is, economics cannot be separated from sexuality, nor sexuality from economics. We treat the land the way we treat women; "we" being dominant males who are historically owners of both.

My articulation of the parallel between issues of land and sexuality is cast in masculine terms and I regret that, but I hope you can translate. I leave the argument in masculine terms because that is the biblical casting of the problem, and because I believe the contemporary problem is still largely machismo. A serious relationship between a man and a woman requires attention to two temptations.[5] On the one hand, there is the temptation to *promiscuity*, so that the woman is used by the man and discarded for the sake of another, i.e., reduced to a commodity. The relation is held casually, and there is no abiding or serious relationship, but only a momentary convenience. On the other hand, there is the temptation to *domination*, so that the woman is held by the man with such an intense commitment that she is owned, controlled, without rights, and so reduced in a different way to a commodity. There are women who are discarded, and there are women who are helplessly and legally dominated, so that they will never be discarded. So also with the land. It can be regarded promiscuously as though it had no significance, and it can be bought, sold, traded, used, discarded as a convenient commodity. Or the land can be held so closely and so tightly, dominated as though it had no rights, until the life is squeezed out of it. In either case, it is as though the land exists for the one who possesses it.

The mystery of an adequate relation with a woman (which we do not often realize) is to hold so loyally as to preclude promiscuity, but to hold so freely as to respect her rights. It is the same with the land. The mystery of faithfulness is to hold the land loyally so as not to reduce it to a commodity, but to hold so freely as to honor its rights as partner and not as possession.

In our society we have terribly distorted relations between men and women, between 'adam and 'adamah, distortions that combine promiscuity and domination, precluding in both cases loyal, freely held covenantal commitments. Likely we shall not correct one of these deathly distortions unless we correct both of them. We shall not have a new land ethic until we have a new sexual ethic, free of both promiscuity and domination. Applied to the land, we shall not have fertility until we have justice toward the land and toward those who depend on the land for life, which means all the brothers and sisters.

II. Sexuality and Economics

The linking of sexuality and economics, of fertility and justice, is evident at many places in the Bible. I will mention two such texts in this preliminary statement, and then a more contemporary observation.

1. Ezek 18:6-8* provides a succinct catalog on what constitutes moral responsibility, i.e., the practice of righteousness that leads to life. Righteousness, according to this catalog, consists in only three elements. Their first is to shun idolatry. The God-questions must be truly discerned so that absolute loyalty is not assigned to any other. Luke Johnson has usefully grasped the economic spin-offs from idolatry, because oppression regularly derives from idolatry.[6] Second, right sexuality is required, so that there is no defilement. The righteous man

> . . . does not defile his neighbor's wife or approach a woman in time of her impurity . . .

Third, the most extended statement concerns economics. The righteous man

> . . . does not oppress anyone, but restores to the debtor his pledge, commits no robbery, gives his bread to the hungry and covers the naked with a garment, does not lend at interest or take any increase . . .

I find it telling that this ethical summary of Ezek 18 derives from idolatry the two decisive ethical questions of sexuality and economics. The first of these is as clear as any conservative could desire, and the second is as extended as any liberal may wish. It would be health-giving in the Church if we agree that every statement on sexuality must be accompanied by one on economics, and conversely. The two are the arenas in which idolatry usually becomes visible. In the language of Wendell Berry, the first concerns how women are treated; the second concerns the treatment of land.

2. Ezek 16:46-50 contains a second remarkable statement related to our theme. The Sodom story of Gen 18–19 is commonly regarded as a statement about homosexuality or gang rape or some such social aberration. The narrative is clearly

about violence in sexual relations. But the Ezekiel text handles this narrative memory with remarkable freedom and imagination. Ezek 16 is a long recital of Israel's history, only now it is not a recital of God's mighty deeds. It is rather a recital of sin, betrayal, and distortion on the part of Israel. It is predictable that the Sodom story might occur in such a recital, but its use by Ezekiel is most surprising. The distortion is now handled in this way:

> There was the guilt of your sister Sodom: she and her daughters had pride, surfeit of food and prosperous ease, but did not aid the poor and needy. They were haughty and did abominable things before me. Therefore I removed them when I saw it (Ezek 16:49-50).

The narrative on sexuality has been recast now as an indictment on economic distortions. The prophet is no doubt inventive. But the prophet is also discerning, for he has seen that sexuality and economic justice are of a piece. The treatments of women and of land are closely paralleled.

3. The third preliminary reference is simply to observe that the great themes of sexuality and economics require us in the contemporary world to pay attention to the insights of Freud and Marx and the interrelatedness of the two. Freud understood that, concerning the mystery of sexuality, we have an endless capacity for distortion and deception. And Marx understood that in economics, self-interest is readily passed off as reality. Marx and Freud were in the end speaking of the same social reality. They understood that modern civilization is grounded in an extraordinary self-deception that distorts both sexuality and economics, and that ends in deep alienation from self, from neighbor, from land.[7]

It is clear that we have become, in all kinds of popular ways, fascinated with Freud. It is equally clear that we are terribly intimidated by the insights of Marx. I submit that in terms of modern categories of criticism, it is the interface of Marx and Freud that will be necessary, urgent, and decisive for the large public problem of sexuality and economics, of productivity and justice. Trying to have Freud without Marx, sexuality without economics, as we mostly do, is an attempt to deal with part of an issue that in fact cannot be separated from its other part. In the end it means we imagine we can have productivity without justice. As long as we entertain that deception, we will not understand how or why Ezekiel transformed the Genesis narrative of sexual violence into a statement about economic abuse. And if we cannot understand that, we shall not have a land policy that avoids both promiscuity and domination.

Against that background, I now want to explore three biblical themes which occur at the interface between sexuality and economics, and which ask about the relation of productivity and justice.

III. The Right of Enclosure

Israel's theory of land, as it is portrayed in the conquest traditions and in the torah provisions, is that the land is assigned to the entire community as a trust from Yahweh. Within the community, clans and "houses" held certain land as entities in the community. This land is regularly designated not as possession but as "inheritance"; that is, the connection between the social unit and the land is inalienable and endures to perpetuity. It need not concern us whether this notion of land was implemented in detail or if it is an imaginative social contract that existed only in theory. What matters is that this is the land theory appropriate to this community, which regarded the land as a gift of God. [8]

Israel's theory of land, deeply rooted in the liberation traditions, clashed with alternative theories and practices that regarded the land as a tradable commodity, not as a gift or trust or inheritance. This alternative land theory [9] (which comes to powerful expression in the tale of Naboth's vineyard in 1 Kings 21) meant that in the real world nobody's land was safe or secure, but that land became an arena for commercialism and all the social problems that emerge when the strong are aligned against the weak. That social relationship of conflict ended, as in the tradition of Amos, with some having a monopoly and others being systematically reduced

to poverty, dependence, and despair.[10] The fundamental
dream of Israel is about land.[11] Israel is a social, theological
experiment in alternative land management. The God of Israel is a God who gives land, and Israel is a people that holds
land in alternative ways. The core tradition is intended to
promote an alternative to the imperial system of land known
both in the Egyptian empire and in the Canaanite city states.[12]

Israel's theory of land as inheritance is practically designed
to resist monopoly and the corresponding social displacement
that is caused by monopoly. In both the torah and in the wisdom instruction, land boundaries are to be maintained as a
fundamental anchor of social policy. Thus in the torah:

> In the inheritance which you will hold in the land that the
> Lord your God gives you to possess, you shall not remove your
> neighbor's landmark, which the men of old have set (Deut
> 19:14).

The language of inheritance[13] is important, but even more
important is the theological grounding of social practice and
social guarantees in Yahweh's will and gift. Social arrangements are legitimated in theological terms.

In wisdom instruction, the prohibition is the same:

> Remove not the ancient landmark which your fathers have
> set. Do you see a man skillful in his work? He will stand be-
> fore kings; He will not stand before obscure men (Prov
> 22:28-29). Do not remove an ancient landmark nor enter the
> fields of the fatherless; for their Redeemer is strong; he will
> plead their cause against you (Prov 23:10-11).

In the first of these two sayings, it is not clear that verse 29
ought to be taken with verse 28. But they are placed together
in the text. Taken that way, the connection between the verses
is interesting, because verse 29 observes that technical skills
are always in the service of the powerful.[14] Applied to verse
28 and with reference to boundary stones, this suggests that
moving boundary stones is not done as a thief in the night,
nor is it a random social practice that anyone may under-
take; rather, it is done through sharp legal practice, shrewd
economics, or cunning court action, whereby the shrewd can
deprive the simple of their patrimony. The practice involves

social "know-how" that is a monopoly of the wise, who are characteristically on the side of the "haves."[15] Their work is systemic and legal, even though socially destructive. Common people, or as verse 28 says, "obscure people," are helpless in the face of such a concentrated, determined technical knowledge.[16]

In the second sapiential prohibition quoted above, the problem of social equality is more obvious because it warns against taking land from orphans, that is, from socially marginal people who have neither connections, means, nor "know-how" to protect their own interests. Indeed, this is why the prophets regularly inveigh against the leadership who "pervert justice" (Amos 5:7, 6:12; Isa 5:7). When the socially powerful pervert justice through legal channels, the "have-nots" who are socially disadvantaged have no recourse. Prov 23:11 is somewhat enigmatic, but the "powerful guardian" (NEB), i.e., an avenger, may indeed be a reference to God, who will not tolerate such violation of land rights, especially if done to the marginal, even if done in socially, legally approved ways. It is striking that on a mundane matter like land boundaries in the literature of Proverbs, such a role is assigned to God.[17]

The most dramatic case of such usurpation is the self-indictment placed in the mouth of the arrogant Assyrian Sennacherib:

> By my own might I have acted, and in my wisdom I have laid my schemes; I have removed the frontiers of nations, and plundered their treasuries (Isa 10:13; cf. Deut 32:8).

Sennacherib is condemned for violation of fixed property boundaries on an international scale. It is probable that the prohibitions in Deuteronomy and Proverbs concern local transactions, but the problem is the same. Now whole nations are cast in the role of the marginal in the face of the Great Power. Seizure of the land of another is an act of exploitative greed and violates God's intent for social order, whether it is local or international. The prohibitions intend to protect the weak against the strong. The development of large landholdings by the rich and powerful is condemned as a betrayal of Israel's most elemental social dream.

These three prohibitions against moving boundaries contain three interesting notes. The first (Deut 19:14) mentions patrimony (so NEB, *naḥalâ*), which bespeaks a certain theory of land and property. The second reference (Prov 22:28-29) is to a contrast between the king and common people, indicating that these innocent-sounding prohibitions are quite discerning statements of social criticism. And the third (Prov 23:10-11) refers specifically to orphans. Taken together, the three articulate a theory of land division that assumes inheritance and the right to hold land, as in the case of an orphan without social power, simply because one is entitled as a member of the community. This view of the land is explicitly contrasted with "royal service" (Prov 22:28), i.e., service in the interest of another theory of land that ignores such entitlements and believes that if there is a concentration of power formidable enough, which can claim legitimacy, moving land markers is simply a legal transaction to secure land for the strong against the weak. This is the theory that operates in the narrative of Naboth's vineyard. Jezebel is unhindered by Israel's egalitarian dream.

The three prohibitions are stated in absolute terms. F.C. Fensham has studied curse provisions in other cultures that concern moving land markers (see n. 16 above). The recurrence of this concern suggests that the matter is foundational for a society. The fact that they are stated as curses indicates that these societies attached to the prohibition the harshest, weightiest religious sanctions available. Society cannot survive when some seize land to which others are entitled simply by being a part of the community, even if the seizure is legally sanctioned.

I want to relate this biblical prohibition on moving land markers to the modern practice of enclosure. By enclosure I mean the legal capacity of more powerful parties to claim exclusive right to a land to the exclusion of the others so that the land can be legally enclosed. Polanyi has studied the dramatic emergence of a theory of market that is related to theories of land. [18] Until the eighteenth century, the market was not held to be autonomous in its operations, but was an aspect of social policy; that is, economic transactions were regarded as part of a larger social network. In that larger network, it was assumed that all parts were related to each other and must in some sense take each other into account. But the emergence of a new theory of autonomous market meant that each party in society was free to do any economic act with respect to neighbors. "Enclosure" is a formidable act that imagines the land and one's possession of it to be unattached to and unconcerned for other social relations. The right of enclosure meant that some could legally keep others off the land. The ones excluded were characteristically the weak and the poor. The policy of enclosure was a radical social change that separated land policy from social interconnectedness and had the effect of further denigrating some to the benefit of others. [19] Polanyi presents the Tudor rulers of England as defenders of the poor against the practice of enclosure. But in the end it was the practice of enclosure that prevailed. That practice embodies the notion that land is privately held without reference to the community. [20]

In a recent, alarming book, Richard Rubenstein judges the policy of land enclosure to be in effect a practice of triage, that is, the intentional elimination of those who are judged to be superfluous, marginal, and not of sufficient value to sustain. [21] Rubenstein then traces the practice of triage into the modern world to more dramatic and obvious matters of social policy and practice. It is crucial to his argument that land enclosure, which excludes some from the land, is in effect triage. Rubenstein's passionate conclusion agrees with the judgment I would make that the Bible in its central social vision opposes policies of land enclosure precisely because they have implicit in them the seeds of triage.

The linkage between enclosure that denies land to some and triage is based on the conviction that one cannot live without land. Everyone must have access to land. (In a mass urban society, everyone must have the social, economic equivalent of land.) It behooves us to recognize that all free-market theory that seeks to separate economic transactions from social relations is destructive, so that the poor (parallel in Berry's reference to women and land) are used and thrown away. The Church must make the case out of its text that such land practice and economic theory—which blatantly serve certain vested interests—are not value-free "laws," but are the practice of visibly destructive values. The reason land markers cannot be moved is because land markers enact and assert social relations that include inalienable guaranteed rights of the weak in the face of the strong, of the poor in the face of the economically powerful.

In Prov 22 the inalienable right of the poor to have land is presented in verse 22 by a warning that is pertinent to our argument:

> Do not rob the poor, because he is poor, do not crush the af-
> flicted at the gate; for Yahweh will plead their cause and de-
> spoil the life of those who despoil them.

It is clear that "robbery" here is not breaking and entering, but is a legal transaction "at the gate."[22] The response of Yahweh to such victimization is that Yahweh will "go to court" on behalf of the poor. This same warning is evident in Prov 23:11: "for their redeemer is strong; he will plead their cause." Yahweh is allied with the poor and will engage in legal defense. It remains in our interpretation to see what this means for contemporary and social practice, but the Israelite commitment against rapacious confiscation seems clear enough. Israel well understood the costs of such policy and practice.

IV. You Shall Not Covet

The second central biblical motif I will explicate is the familiar tenth commandment "You shall not covet" (Exod 20:17, Deut 5:21).[23] That commandment has been largely trivialized into a psychological matter concerning jealousy and envy. Marvin Cheney has most persuasively argued that the commandment does not refer to such matters that may vex the "introspective conscience of the West," but is to be understood in terms of public policy and social practice.[24] Cheney concludes that the commandment concerns especially land policy: "Do not covet your neighbor's field." In terms

of our governing parallel between land and women, it is
worth noting that the second most important matter is, "You
shall not covet your neighbor's wife." It is wife and land that
are crucial to the ordering of the community. Moreover, it
is plausible to suggest that this tenth commandment cor-
responds in a special way to the first commandment, "You
shall have no other gods." Yahweh, unlike other gods in the
Near East, is holy, and therefore beyond location, and acts
in freedom.[25] The counterpart to that radical character of
God who may not be reduced in idolatrous ways is the dignity and worth of the neighbor. That respect for neighbor
comes to its climactic expression in the maintenance of and
respect for land and house. Insofar as the tenth commandment is related to the first, we have a structure not unlike
Ezek 18:6-9, which moves from idolatry into matters of sexuality and economics. Cheney concludes that this prohibition on coveting concerns land management and land
ownership. The rapacious land policies of the monarchy (as
in 1 Kings 21) permitted and legitimated confiscation of a
most greedy and destructive kind.[26] The Israelite vision of
social organization, articulated by this commandment, is to
prevent such confiscation that takes from the defenseless poor
who have no economic or legal means to protect themselves
against the economically powerful.

Perhaps the two most important exegetical comments on
this commandment are in prophetic oracles from Micah and
Isaiah. These two prophets most consistently critique the royal
apparatus in Jerusalem, which is to be understood, among
other things, as an embodiment of land surplus, if not monopoly.[27]

Mic 2:1-5 begins in verses 1-2 as a sapiential statement
simply observing the predictable consequences of land seizure. But then in verses 3-5, the poetry takes a more severe
prophetic tone with a double "therefore," laying out the consequences of such land seizure:

> Therefore thus says the Lord: behold, against this family I
> am devising evil, from which you cannot remove your necks;
> and you shall not walk haughtily, for it will be an evil time.

> In that day they shall take up a taunt song against you, and
> wail with bitter lamentation, and say, "We are utterly ruined:
> he changes the portion of my people; how he removes it from
> me! Among our captors he divides our fields." Therefore you
> will have none to cast the line by lot in the assembly of the
> Lord.

The first two verses concern scheming and calculation that
amount to sharp, exploitative business dealing. The "woe"
asserts that those who manage to grab land from others will
surely come to death. [28] That in itself is a remarkable statement. Then the "therefore" statements of threat correspond
to the violations. [29] Those who devised evil now have Yahweh devise evil against them. Now there is a reaping of what
has been sown.

Finally, according to Israelite faith, Yahweh must be reck-
oned with and answered to for the way land is managed.
There is no escape from this accountability. Those who have
so much land that is not rightly theirs, even if legally secured,
will come to destruction. Others will come and divide their
fields. In context the poetry presumably refers to the Assyri-
ans. The Bible insists that undisciplined and unneighborly
land practice finally leads to a reckoning. The extreme case
among us is the Somozan land in Nicaragua, which, sooner
or later, will be divided. [30] But we would do well to think
through the social dynamics closer to home. The Bible articulates a remarkable theory of how the historical process works,
because that process is governed by Yahweh. In our postmodern culture, we must see if these same realities must still
be heeded.

The end result in verse 5 says simply, "Therefore you will
have none to cast the line by lot in the assembly of Yahweh."
Albrecht Alt has argued that this poetic statement anticipates
that there will come a time when the adherents of Yahweh,
the ones blessed by Yahweh (perhaps the meek), will meet
in public assembly to redistribute the land. [31] That assembly,
in the name of the liberating, covenanting God, will be a
meeting of peasants entitled to their patrimony. [32] The big
land-grabbers will not be present when the boundary lines
are redrawn. Indeed, the land-grabbers will not even be ad-

mitted to the meeting and so will end up landless. Now this may sound like an extreme social vision, but it is the vision that is being acted out in revolutionary ways in many parts of our world. This is a vision of a complete inversion, in which coveting as social policy comes to its sorry end. In a quite concrete way, the first will become last and the last will finally be first. That terse formula is, among other things, a theory of land distribution (see Mark 10:31 in context).

Isa 5:8-10 closely parallels the Micah passage. This text also begins with "woe:"[33]

> Woe to those who join house to house, who add field to field, until there is no more room, and you are made to dwell alone in the midst of the land. The Lord of hosts has sworn in my hearing: Surely many houses shall be desolate, large and beautiful houses, without inhabitant. For ten acres of vineyard shall yield one bath, and a homer of seed shall yield but an ephah.

The warning is against buying up large tracts of land and therefore displacing peasants who have lived on the land. Verse 9 departs from the "woe" form (as did Mic 2:3-4) in order to announce Yahweh's immediate engagement on the side of the dispossessed. This great concentration of wealth will come to a sorry end, because it cannot be sustained against the intent of Yahweh who opposes monopoly and is inclined toward egalitarianism. Thus the large houses will be terminated. And, finally, in verse 10 we have a consequence that is of interest for our juxtaposition of justice and fertility. Ten acres will yield only a little. The land will not yield as it is expected to do. Land that is handled unjustly will finally not be productive. "Bath" and "ephah" are measures of grain. This land will be short on produce. Because the Bible does not speak in terms of secondary causation, it does not comment on or explain the reasoning that leads to this conclusion. We are not told why or in what way injustice works against productivity. But in broad sweep, it is sufficient to know that where there is injustice, there will sooner or later be infertility. The connection between justice and fertility is invisible and never well-explicated. But it must be noted that for ancient Israel, just social relations are foundational and prerequisite for productive land.

This latter point is dramatically stated in Hos 4:1-3. Every part of this brief poetic unit concerns land. It begins with a summons to court concerning the inhabitants of the land (v. 1a). It indicts the community for violating torah, because there is no knowledge of God in the land (vv. 1b-2). It concludes with an announcement that the land has severe drought until the reliable structures and systems of life are destroyed. It is astonishing that the poet dares to say that failure to keep torah leads to life-destroying drought. Failure to practice justice makes fertility impossible.

I wish to cite only one other text that may illuminate the matter of coveting as a systemic practice of the strong against the weak. In the well-known narrative of 2 Sam 11, David covets Bathsheba, wife of Uriah, and takes possession of her. He covets and seizes. He regards this woman as something to use and abuse. The connection to our theme is in the prophetic parable of Nathan in 2 Sam 12:1-4. Nathan's parable gives a close reading of David's "conquest" [sic]. It is a rich man and a poor man, one who had much and one who had little. The parable is pliable. It can, as Nathan intends, be linked to sexual conquests. But it could as easily refer to land, concerning those who have little and those who have much. The operational verb is "take" (*laqah*, see 11:4 and Nathan's indictment in 12:9). In 1 Kgs 21:19, the verbs are different (*rasah, yarash*), but the questions concerning land are the same. Thus the parable mediates between land and sexuality, between field (Naboth) and wife (David). Both forms of coveting will finally destroy.[34]

V. DEFILEMENT OF LAND

The third theme I will pursue is more radical and more difficult to handle. It is defilement of land. The reason this is such a difficult theme is that ritual defilement is a notion quite alien to us. Now we are in the sphere of shame and contamination that is much more elemental than guilt and morality.[35] Such defilement renders its object impure, unavailable for religious use. The holy God of Israel will not and cannot stay in a place that is defiled.

The text that is my point of reference is Deut 24:1-4. This law concerns marital relations. It is about a situation in which a man divorces a wife. She goes to a second husband. But the second marriage also ends. Then she wants to return to the first husband and resume that relation. The point of the legal prohibition is that the first husband, even if he wants to, may not take the woman back again. (Notice that in verse 4 we again have the word "take," *laqaḥ*. The reason that such a return is prohibited is that she is "defiled" *(time')*. That is, she was intended for this singular "use" of the first husband. But having been put to other use, i.e., the second husband, she is no longer suitable for the first, proper relation. Now this may strike us as primitive and severely sexist, for matters are clearly not symmetrical for the man and the woman. But on its own terms, one may consider this defilement. The prohibition refers to improper use that renders proper use impossible. The improper use is to be engaged for something other than intended use.

The Deuteronomic theological commentary on this prohibition in verse 4b makes an important move in interpretation:

> . . . for that is an abomination before the Lord, and you shall not bring guilt upon the land which the Lord your God gives you for an inheritance.

First, the commentary labels the second relationship an abomination, which means a distortion that endangers the entire community.[36] We may say such marital maneuvering may threaten social solidarity and order, but the usage attributes an almost material notion of abomination, as though a substance of destruction is thereby introduced into the community.

The other theological comment interests us most directly. Such an act will bring guilt on the land of inheritance. The distorted marital relation causes distortion of the land. Moreover, the land is *nahalah*, that is, land that is a trust made

according to the promise of Yahweh. Distorted marriage relation leads to distorted land. The ritual language of contamination makes the land less than productive, i.e., under curse,
a place where God will not grant fertility.

It is a matter of great interest that this text is utilized by
Jeremiah in 3:1ff. [37] Jeremiah lived at a moment when Judah
was to be exiled and lose its land. Jeremiah is preoccupied
with the matter of land and land loss, and presents an argument about how land is lost. [38] In this poetry the prophet takes
the law of Deut 24:1-4 as a metaphor. In this usage Yahweh
is the first husband who has been violated by the wife, Judah.
Judah the wife has been rejected in infidelity, and so she goes
to a second husband, presumably Assyrian alliance and
Canaanite religion. But those connections do not work, so
Judah wishes to return to Yahweh, to reestablish the covenant relation with God. The torah precludes that resump-
tion of relation, however. Yahweh is prevented by the torah
from taking back Judah, even if Yahweh had chosen or wished
to do so.

Two points interest us here. First, Yahweh is willing to
violate the torah prohibition for the sake of the relation.
Against the torah, Yahweh yearns for a restoration. Against
the torah, Yahweh urges Israel to repent and come home (Jer
3:12, 14; 4:1-2). Notice that in Jer 4:3-4, agricultural images
are used for criteria of return as in Hos 10:12.

The second item that concerns us is that the language of
defilement is used by Jeremiah, as in the old teaching of Deuteronomy:

> Would not that land be greatly polluted (3:1, see 2:7, 23)?
> You have polluted the land in your vile harlotry (3:2).

The language of defilement is used to portray distorted covenant. That language concerns the relation with Yahweh. But
at the same time, that language is used to characterize the
situation of the land and its social organization. The land has
now been treated so that it is not productive. And this in turn
is because Yahweh refuses to stay in such a place or to grant
blessings of fertility in such a context.

The language of *ritual contamination* is an important one

for speaking about land abuse.[39] I suggest four dimensions of the problem vis-a-vis a holy God and holy ground:

a) The language of defilement and contamination is probably what is operative in much of the current conversation about sexuality, with particular reference to homosexuality, escalated even more with the current panic about AIDS. That is, the enormous passion against acceptance of homosexuality and fear of it appear to be a sense of uncleanness that endangers the entire community and "pollutes the land," endangering everyone. The reaction indicates that something more profound and elemental than guilt or moral outrage is at work. The response is of the depth to show that this social phenomenon is perceived as endangering the entire community.

b) More concretely, there is no doubt that chemicals (particularly fertilizer) contaminate the land, threaten the water table, and eventually endanger the productivity of the soil.

c) It is striking that we refer to nuclear fallout as "pollution" and contamination, and that we speak of "dirty bombs" that so defile the earth as to make life impossible except in its lowest forms.

d) Taken all together, the technology of contamination may create a moral situation in which the possibility of life is jeopardized. That, in fact, is what the priestly tradition in the Old Testament is about.[40] An ethic of "use, abuse, discard" is evident in every area of life. In terms of land and sexuality, matters of wrong use (injustice) threaten fertility and productivity. In our secular mode we would not speak of it so, but such a practice eventually will make the earth a place where God cannot and will not abide. At least we might say that the "power for life" may be withdrawn. And where that happens, productivity ends. It is clear that a land ethic that uses, abuses, and discards is a practice of pollution and fickleness. It creates a fundamental cleavage between a Creator who wills life and a creation that squanders and finally rejects life.

These three themes together—*moving boundaries*, which translates into the practice of enclosure; *coveting*, which we understand as rapacious land policy; and *defilement*, which we understand as pollution of the ecosystem of life—are ways in which the Bible speaks about land management. These three themes respectively concern geographic, economic, and ritual dimensions of life. All of them together articulate policies that end in death. Death is caused where boundary markers abuse the poor and God's vengeance is evoked. Death is caused where coveting becomes policy and the poor are displaced and despoiled. Death is caused when defilement is practiced that causes the power for life to be withdrawn. The conversation in ancient Israel (which we must continue) is whether the way we relate to the land is a way of death. The staggering discernment is that death comes not only to the weak and poor who are victims of such policies and values, but eventually death reaches even into the life of the powerful and affluent who are not immune to death when it comes to the community (see e.g., Exod 11:4-6).

VI. Land Management

Finally, the Bible affirms that land can be managed in ways that give life. It does not need to be handled toward death. The Bible is not a warning or a threat, but an invitation to another way. It is, however, an invitation that requires a break with the death systems that encompass us. Let me review briefly three texts that are related to our three themes.

1. Against moving boundaries and enclosure systems, the Bible celebrates the old land theory of *inalienable patrimony*. The text I cite is Jer 32:1-15. In that text (which is commonly regarded as having an historical basis), the prophet is summoned directly by God to purchase the land. The occasion of the summons is that the Babylonian armies are invading and the economic system is collapsing. But the summons from Yahweh is based on the conviction that the old inheritance rights finally will prevail. Even the great empire is not free to move boundaries and claim land against those old tribal claims. The careful language of the mandate is to exercise the "right of redemption by purchase" *(mispaṭ haggéulah legnôth*, v. 7) and "right of possession and redemption" *(mispat hayerûsah, . . . haggéullah Qenah*, v. 8). The

transaction is done in precise legal terms, with great care to secure clear title. Even the mandate from Yahweh is expressed in those categories. [41] But the theological claim of the narrative is the oracle in verse 15: "Houses and fields and vineyards shall again be bought *(gnn)* in this land." The economy will be reestablished. And when the economy is reestablished after the current debacle, the old rights will prevail. (The argument is parallel to that in Mic 2:5. In both cases, the old tribal basis of land will endure after the current imperial rapaciousness.) Those who violate those old rights in the interest of land speculation and land seizure will not prevail. The text seems to assume an economic retribalization against the more recent concentration of wealth in the hands of few, either foreign or Israel's own elite.

2. Against coveting, Israel celebrates land redistribution, which breaks up monopolies and gives back land to those who should properly have it. In Josh 13–19, care is taken that tribal groups receive their proper entitlements. In Josh 7–8, the text knowingly observes that this practice of patrimonial land is threatened by Achan's sin, which holds goods apart from the community. But the narrative of Achan's sin is only a candid footnote to the main textual tradition of land division. According to the stylized claims of the tradition, the land is held in alternative ways. [42]

That land division from the Joshua text was obliterated by royal patterns that violated such covenantal guarantees. The Davidic house ignored and destroyed old tribal land arrangements. In the later anticipation of Ezek 47:13–48:29, the land memory of Josh 13–19 becomes a prototype for the land apportionment to come. The way the land was remembered in Joshua becomes the way it is expected in Ezekiel. Micah 2:1-5 had anticipated a new land division. And now Ezekiel speaks after the long generations of the monarchal system, after the failure of that system in 587, and after the exile without land. Ezek 47–48 shows the old memories coming to fresh fruition. The report of this anticipation in Ezekiel is obviously much too stylized and artificial to be regarded in terms of an actual policy action. But the text does show that Israel believes present land arrangements are an unfortunate development that are not secure in the future. In the coming time, the land will be reapportioned according to the old, enduring promises. The promises speak authoritatively against current practice.

The land will indeed be redistributed. This relates to the practice of the Jubilee Year, which consists of returning land to its rightful owner (Lev 25). The land is not managed according to calculating economic transactions. There may be such transactions, but they happen in contexts of promise and inheritance, which finally override such transactions. It is worth noting that that powerful tradition of land redistribution can be understood as the center of Luke's presentation of Jesus. [43] Jesus is a threat to vested interests in his time because he proposed to give land and dignity back to those who had lost it. I judge such matters to be important among us because the great revolutions of our time against colonial power are in fact an effort to redistribute land according to tribal conventions that have been gravely distorted in the interest of concentrated surplus. It will not do to dismiss as terrorist or communist those who insist on implementing the old promissory land management in the face of present settlements based on seizure.

3. Against defilement and abomination, the Bible anticipates a time when the land is free of such contamination so that production can be full and the blessings of life abundantly available. Two prophetic texts may be cited. Hos 2:21-23 is an answer to Hos 5:3; 6:10. In 5:3 and 6:10, Israel's covenantal violations have polluted the land:

> For now, O Ephraim, you have played the harlot. Israel is defiled. . . . In the house of Israel I have seen a horrible thing; Ephraim's harlotry is there, Israel is defiled (5:3; 6:10).

In both cases, land defilement is expressed in the metaphors of fickleness and harlotry.

In the great poems of Hos 2:2-23, the land will function again, after it has ceased to function. [44] And then, in a lyrical portrayal of new creation, the poet says:

> In that day, says the Lord, I will answer the heavens, and they shall answer the earth; and the earth shall answer the

> grain, the wine, and the oil, and they shall answer Jezreel,
> and I will sow him for myself in the land.

The restored land is a conversation of productivity in which all parts will gladly respond to each other, and the land will bear an abundance of grain, wine, and oil. But that will happen only where the defilements and harlotries are overcome by a season of exile-landlessness. It is after exile that this faithful God will say,

> And I will have pity on Not pitied, and I will say to Not my people, "You are my people," and he shall say, "Thou art my God" (v. 23).

The other text related to defilement and restoration is Isa 62:4-5, which is an answer to Isa 6:5. In that first familiar text, the prophet says, "I am defiled and I live among defiled people." The Book of Isaiah asserts that judgment comes against such massive defilement. But then in 62:4-5, after the judgment and exile and loss of land, the lyrics again assert the coming fullness of productivity:

> You shall no more be termed Forsaken, and your land shall no more be termed Desolate, but you shall be called My delight is in her, and your land Married; For the Lord delights in you, and your land shall be married. For as a young man marries a virgin, so shall your sons marry you, and as a bridegroom rejoices over the bride, so shall your God rejoice over you.

It is amazing that in verse 4 land is referred to three times:

> Your land shall no more be termed desolate, Your land married, Your land married.

The term "married is be'ûlah, which is derived from ba'al and means "fructified," "made productive." The statements about land are surrounded in verses 4a and 5 with marriage images: You will no more be termed divorced, abandoned . . . in verse 5 the metaphor concerns human marriage (twice), and then offers joy as the joy of a wedding.

In all these cases the power is overcome. The laws of patrimony prevail against moving boundaries (Jer 32:1-15). Land redistribution overcomes coveting, which leads to inequality (Ezek 47:13–48:29). Productivity recurs in a land marked by defilement (Hos 2:21-23). The land will again be home. It does not happen simply by divine fiat, but only by historical activity that is risky and costly.

I suggest that this analysis provides a grid of three pairs of themes:

> *enclosure . . . inalienable patrimony* (Jer 32:1-15), *coveting . . . redistribution* (Ezek 47:13–48:29), *defilement . . . fertility restored* (Hos 2:21-23; Isa 62:4-5).

These are ways of life and death. We must ponder that the ways of enclosure, coveting, and contamination have become acceptable policy among us. Now we are at a crisis point. The text reintroduces to us the non-negotiable conditions of life in the land. We hold a view of land that we know has pertinence to public conversation. We are at a place in our society when we must re-ask foundational questions about use, abuse, and discarding. The alternative mediated in these texts is to "tend and care," to caress and cherish (Gen 2:15). But that work requires a break with an ethic of monopoly and surplus value. It is a costly repentance. So the prophet Jeremiah can say:

> If you return, O Israel, says the Lord, to me you should return. If you remove your abominations from my presence, and do not waver, and if you swear, "As the Lord lives," in truth, in justice, and in uprightness, then the nations shall bless themselves in him, and in him they shall glory (Jer 4:1-2).

For thus says the Lord to the men of Judah and to the inhabitants of Jerusalem:

> Break up your fallow ground, and sow not among the thorns. Circumcise yourselves to the Lord, remove the foreskin of your hearts, O men of Judah and inhabitants of Jerusalem; lest my wrath go forth like fire, and burn with none to quench it, because of the evil of your doings (Jer 4:3-4).

There is in this poem a massive condition of "if-then," and it is presented as an agricultural metaphor. The poet invites Judah to a repentant life in the land in order to avoid the fire. The human, covenantal issues do not admit of technical solution. Land management must be restored to its place in the fabric of social relations. Productivity requires attention to justice. Fertility causes us to rethink economics. Sexuality raises questions of righteousness. Without righteousness and justice in land management, there may come a destroyer who will "make your land a waste (Jer 4:7). It need not be so. But it can happen, and is indeed happening before our very eyes.

1. Phyllis Trible, *God and the Rhetoric of Sexuality* (Philadelphia: Fortress Press, 1978), p. 78, shrewdly names 'adam as "the earth creature," in order to underscore the relation to earth. Moreover, Trible rightly sees that 'adamah has priority over 'adam in the creation narrative.

2. The relation of covenant and creation is not without problem in current Old Testament theology. Nonetheless, Karl Barth, *Church Dogmatics* III, 1, (Edinburgh: T. and T. Clark, 1958) has wisely seen that the two themes are integrally related to each other. The juxtaposition of the two is necessary to see that humankind has a covenantal relation with creation.

3. Wendell Berry, *Recollected Essays 1965–80* (San Francisco: North Point Press, 1981), p. 215.

4. *Ibid.*, p. 191.

5. Abraham Heschel, *Who is Man?* (Stanford: Stanford University Press, 1965) has characterized human life when there is a loss of transcendence. Everyone then is a tool to be used, and is reduced to usefulness. Phyllis Trible, *Texts of Terror* (Philadelphia: Fortress Press, 1984) has explicated in a most discerning way biblical texts in which women are subjected to promiscuity and domination.

* Bible quotations are from the Revised Standard Version (RSV) unless indicated otherwise.

6. Luke T. Johnson, *Sharing Possessions* (Philadelphia: Fortress Press, 1981), pp. 84–95 and *passim*, has a remarkable analysis of the interrelation between idolatry, possessiveness, and oppression.

7. Erich Fromm, *Escape From Freedom* (New York: Farrar and Rinehart, 1941), and *The Anatomy of Human Destructiveness* (New York: Holt, Rinehart, and Winston, 1973), has most discerningly reflected on the interrelatedness of the themes of Marx and Freud. For a suggestion on the common rootage of their concern, see John M. Cuddihy, *The Ordeal of Civility* (New York: Basic Books, 1974).

8. Norman Gottwald, *The Tribes of Yahweh* (Maryknoll, N.Y.: 1979) has most sharply articulated the socio-economic foundations and implications of this alternative notion of land. Clearly there is nothing romantic in such a view of land, but it has profound and serious social implications that can only be regarded as subversive.

9. See Robert B. Coote, *Amos Among the Prophets* (Philadelphia: Fortress, 1981), pp. 24–25.

10. On the intentional management of such poverty, see Bernard Lang, "The Social Organization of Peasant Poverty in Biblical Israel," *Journal for the Study of the Old Testament* (JSOT) 24 (1982), pp. 47–63.

11. On my own exposition of the theme see Walter Brueggemann, *The Land* (Philadelphia: Fortress Press, 1977).

12. On the "core tradition" see Walter Harrelson, "Life, Faith, and the Emergence of Tradition," *Tradition and Theology in the Old Testament* ed. by Douglas A. Knight (Philadelphia: Fortress Press, 1977), pp. 11–30, and Norman K. Gottwald, *The Hebrew Bible, A Socio-Literary Introduction* (Philadelphia: Fortress Press, 1985), p. 144.

13. See particularly the New English Bible translation of this passage. The term here rendered "inheritance" is there rendered as "patrimony," a term more telling for a theory of land possession.

14. The text contrasts kings with "hidden" people *(ḥšk)*. The Revised Standard Version (RSV) renders as "obscure," the New English Bible (NEB) as "common." In this context, the contrast suggests people who have no public visibility, no social power, and so who have no chance for "the pursuit of happiness."

15. On the interplay of technical wisdom and established political interest, see Glendon E. Bryce, *A Legacy of Wisdom* (Lewisburg: Bucknell University Press, 1979) chapters 6–7, and George E. Mendenhall, "The Shady Side of Wisdom: The Date and Purpose of Genesis 3," *A Light Unto My Path*, ed. by Howard N. Bream, Ralph D. Heim, Carey A. Moore (Philadelphia: Fortress Press, 1974), pp. 319–34.

16. F. C. Fensham "Common Trends in Curses of the Near Eastern Treaties" and *Kudurru* "Inscriptions Compared with Maledictions of Amos and Isaiah," ZAW 75 (1963), pp. 155–75 has summarized the data on curses related to the movement of boundaries. The use of curse formulae suggests that such religious sanction is the only force available to those who have no social power.

17. It is instructive that the Revised Standard Version capitalizes "Redeemer," thus interpreting unambiguously with reference to God. That the text speaks so of God may suggest a connection to Job 19:25 and the appeal there to a redeemer. Both texts, in very different contexts, raise the question of theodicy.

18. Kari Polanyi, *The Great Transformation* (Boston: Beacon Press, 1944).

19. *Ibid.*, p. 78. Polanyi cites a key decision made at Speenhamland, England, one that was pivotal in repositioning the poor in the network

of social relation. This particular case cited by Polanyi indicates that the issue of theodicy is not a general speculative issue, but relates to quite concrete questions of social policy and practice.

20. One may regard Deut 24:19-22 as an Israelite articulation against the practice of enclosure. The land must be left open for those not "in possession."

21. Richard Rubenstein, *The Age of Triage* (Boston: Beacon Press, 1983).

22. On the "gate" as a social institution, see Ludwig Koehler, *Hebrew Man* Nashville: Abingdon Press, 1957), pp. 127–50. References to "the gate" show that the act against the poor is systematic and institutional.

23. On this commandment, see the fine introduction by Walter Harrelson, *The Ten Commandments and Human Rights* (Philadelphia: Fortress Press, 1980), pp. 148–54.

24. Marvin L. Cheney, "You Shall Not Covet Your Neighbor's House," *Pacific Theological Review* 15 (Winter 1982), pp. 3–13. The formula on "introspective conscience" is from Krister Stendahl, "The Apostle Paul and the Introspective Conscience of the West," *Harvard Theological Review* (HTR 56 (1963), pp. 199–215.

25. Cyrus Gordon, "A Note on the Tenth Commandment," *Journal of Bible and Religion* 31 (1963), pp. 208–9, has suggested that the tenth commandment is derived from the character of Yahweh, because Yahweh is unlike the other gods of Canaan who covet. Such a theological contrast with other gods helps link the commandment to the fundamental claims of Yahwism.

26. On the dimension of monarchy, note that Gottwald, *The Hebrew Bible*, p. 293, refers to the monarchy as "Israel's Counterrevolutionary Establishment." Clearly Gottwald intends that "counterrevolutionary" apply to socio-economic matters such as land policy. In parallel fashion, Mendenhall's "The Monarchy," *Interpretation* 29 (1975), pp. 155–70 refers to the monarchy as the "paganization" and Canaanization" of Israel. This also applies to questions of egalitarianism in economic relations.

27. See Mendenhall, "The Shady Side," cited in n. 15 above, on the monopoly of knowledge that supports a monopoly of technology, which soon leads to a monopoly of wealth.

28. See Klaus Koch, "Is There a Doctrine of Retribution in the Old Testament?" *Theodicy in the Old Testament*, ed. by James L. Crenshaw (Philadelphia: Fortress Press, 1983), pp. 57–87, on the certitude with which consequences follow deeds. The "woe" form does not assert an active agent in punishment, but only that such outcomes inexorably follow such actions. Thus land grabbing does not depend on the action of God for retribution, but yields its own destructive consequences. One cannot land-grab, so the poem argues, with impunity.

29. On this correspondence, see Patrick D. Miller, *Sin and Judgment in the Prophets* (Chico, Calif.: Scholars Press, 1982), and specifically on this text, pp. 29–31.

30. On the inevitability of this social movement, see Walter LaFeber *Inevitable Revolutions* (New York: Norton, 1983).

31. Albrecht Alt, "Micah 2:1-5 Ges Anadasmos in Judah," *Kleine Schriften zur Geschichte des Volkes Israel* III (München: C.H. Beck, 1959), pp. 373–81.

32. On the sociology of Micah, see the suggestive statement of Hans Walter Wolff, "Micah the Moreshite—The Prophet and His Background." *Israelite Wisdom*, ed. by John G. Gammie (Missoula: Scholars Press, 1978), pp. 77–84.

33. On this passage and the "woe" form, see William Whedbee, *Isaiah and Wisdom* (Nashville: Abingdon Press, 1971), pp. 93–98.

34. Gottwald, *The Hebrew Bible*, p. 210, offers an exposition of the commandment, which relates it to land policy.

35. On the elemental character of shame that is more foundational than guilt, see Erik Erikson, *Identity and the Life Cycle* (New York: International Universities Press, 1959), pp. 65–82, and Paul Ricoeur, *The Symbolism of Evil* (New York: Harper, 1967).

36. On the meaning of "abomination" in Deuteronomy, see Jean L'Hour, "Les Interdits toébadans le Deuteronome," *Revue Biblique* (RB) 71 (1964), pp. 481–503.

37. For one proposal concerning the relation of these texts, see T. R. Hobbs, "Jeremiah 3:1-5 and Deuteronomy 24:1-4," *Zeitschrift für die Alttestamentliche Wissenschaft* (ZAW) 86 (1974), pp. 23–29.

38. On the motif of land in the tradition of Jeremiah, see Walter Brueggemann, "Israel's Sense of Place in Jeremiah," *Rhetorical Criticism*, ed. by Jared J. Jackson and Martin Kessler (Pittsburgh: Pickwick Press, 1974), pp. 149–65, and John Bracke, "The Coherence and Theology of Jeremiah 30–31," (Unpublished Dissertation, Union Theological Seminary, Richmond, Va., 1983), especially chapter 3.

39. On land and its contamination as a religious-cultural problem, see Mary Douglas, *Purity and Danger* (London: Routledge and Kegon Paul, 1966).

40. See Fernando Belo, *A Materialistic Reading of the Gospel of Mark* (Maryknoll, N.Y.: Orbis Books, 1981) for a consideration of the sociology of purity.

41. On the relation of this passage to the issue of theodicy as a social problem, see Walter Brueggemann, "Theodicy in a Social Dimension," forthcoming in JSOT.

42. It is telling that in the Book of Joshua, it is Rahab the harlot who is instrumental in the well-being of Israel and the downfall of Jericho. Jericho is clearly a walled city that embodies the "Canaanite" monopoly against which Israel is mobilized. It is therefore expected that such a marginal person should be on the side of those who assault the monopoly. A great deal will be discerned in such narratives when we read with sociological sensitivity. Gottwald, *The Hebrew Bible*, pp. 258–59, in speaking

of the social location of Rahab says that the narrative "never ceases to emphasize how much of the 'outside,' both communally and territorially, is 'inside' Israel."

43. See Sharon Ringe, *Jesus, Liberation, and the Jubilee Year*, (Philadelphia: Fortress Press, 1985).

44. On the structural reversal in this poem, see David J. A. Cline's "Hosea 2: Structure and Interpretation," *Studia Biblica 1978*, JSOT Supp. II (Sheffield: University of Sheffield, 1979), pp. 83–103.

3

Implications of a New Land Ethic

C. Dean Freudenberger

Today we recognize that alongside consultations on nuclear disarmament, the question being addressed by this Theology of Land Project is of equal concern. This point cannot be over-stressed. If we do not develop a new theology, ethic, and so-cial attitude about the land (social ethos), whether it be from nuclear incineration, nuclear winter, or desertification as a consequence of human abuse, the end result will be the same—another lifeless planet within our galaxy. One comes to this kind of conclusion after spending thirty years at work in agricultural development for food production across the six continents of this planet. This conclusion is not drawn from the logic of library research. What we are talking about, us-ing the words of Carl Sagan and Rolf Knierim, is of "cosmic importance."[1] The fundamental question facing the par-ticipants in this project is simply this: from where will come the impetus for this new theology, ethic and ethos? As far as I can observe, it will have to come from the religious com-munities.

The four questions addressed by this Theology of Land Project will provide the structure for this article. It is my hope that this article will contribute to an understanding of how theological and ethical constructs enable us to judge and envision in relation to specific social and technical questions that are demanding our response. These questions include such issues as land ownership, farm policy, rural community, agricultural research and technology, and foreign policy.

I. What is the prevalent land ethic operative in the United States, and what are the effects?

Because of the historically unprecedented magnitude of our farm crisis, as well as the food and environmental crisis that has spread across the face of the entire globe, and the need to communicate clearly at this critical time, it is necessary to be as candid as possible. My response to the first part of this question is as follows.

The prevalent land ethic operative in this nation can be defined as an "ethic" of profit-taking. This is to say that "the good" is understood in our society to be related to wealth accumulation. A "good" farmer is a wealthy and prosperous farmer. A "bad" farmer is a bankrupt farmer. A "good" agricultural system is a wealth-generating system. Within this "ethical" frame of reference, efficiency in crop production is a primary standard of measurement. For many years, agricultural research has been devoted to this measure. When I was a student attending the California State Polytechnic College of Agriculture at San Luis Obispo from 1948 to 1952, I was trained within this assumption context. It took me almost twenty years to begin to understand that this was a cul-de-sac of massive proportion. The maximization of yields per acre has been the norm within this limited measure, even though the bottom-line figure on the ledger sheet about fiscal profit and loss was, of course, the ultimate measure of good and bad. This so-called "ethic" and measure of progress is mechanistic, materialistic, reductionistic, dualistic, anthropocentric, and Machiavellian. Within the construct of this measure is the value of the free market system and the idea that private land ownership provides license to do as one pleases with the land. This, candidly, is the common denominator of the prevalent land "ethic" operative in our society today.

The consequences of this ethic of profit-taking and wealth generation are many. The most serious one is that of a truncated United States federal and state agricultural research agenda within the research establishment of the land-grant colleges and private agribusiness institutions. The work of Busch and Lacy, in their book *Science, Agriculture, and the Politics of Research*, is awesomely clarifying on this point. [2] Of equal clarity is the Dillman and Hobbs book *Rural Society in the U.S.: Issues for the 1980s*. [3] The agricultural research establishment in this nation is now irresponsibly truncated as a consequence of the operative land ethic in this nation at this time. We need to be on the alert for the upcoming publication by Professor Kenneth Dahlberg (editor) on *Evaluation of Agricultural Research: The Choice of Evaluative Concepts and Indicators in Their Relation to National Goals*. [4] This project was sponsored by the National Endowment for the Humanities and the National Science Foundation for the purpose of providing federal agencies with new criteria for evaluating agricultural research proposals. We are all clearly aware of the chaos in our present farm crisis; there is no need to go through the litany again. [5] The point to be made at this moment is that our crisis is a result of a misconstrued land ethic. Other consequences must be listed: (a) the loss of agricultural leadership, (b) a shipwrecked history of United States farm policy, (c) a threatened United States food security system, (d) paralysis in the development of a world food security system, (e) a bankruptcy of our farm families and rural communities, (f) the awesome loss suffered in soil erosion, water resource loss and pollution, (g) genetic diversity truncation, (h) the build-up of toxic agro-petrochemicals in soil and water deposits, (i) atmospheric pollutant fallout on crop and forest land, and (j), using the words of E. F. Schumacher, the disinheritance of future generations and the erosion of our self-understanding of what it means to be human in terms of relationships to each other and to all life and its resource base of the whole of creation . . . of our relationships to the common heritage of the land.[6]

II. BASED UPON BIBLICAL REFLECTIONS, WHAT DO YOU THINK A SOUND THEOLOGY OF THE LAND SHOULD CONSIST OF?

I am not a theologian nor a biblical scholar. However, I am a colleague on a faculty at a school of theology. If it were not for this nurturing and tutoring setting in which I work, I would not want to try my hand at responding to this question. But since my working context on a theological faculty and the growing necessity facing me of dealing with this question, I give it a try. In the process, I encourage all of us to make the endeavor.

Basic to our theological formulation about any issue is the question: What informs our theology? We all have a similar answer that is worthy of reflection. We work from our faith heritage in the Bible, in our heritage of experience within our Christian religious community, in our own experiences of our own historical contexts, and with our facilities of reflection and reasoning. I work out of my experiences of service and observation as an agronomist/ethicist in all of Africa, most of Southeast Asia, part of Latin America, the Pacific island communities, the Caribbean, my own country, and parts of western Canada. Out of this experiential context, with a focus on agriculture, I reflect upon my faith experience and heritage. Most specifically, with the help of several of my faculty colleagues, I have been led to study the recent works dealing with the theology and ethics of the land—works of Walter Brueggemann, Claus Westermann, Rolf Knierim, Odil Steck, Von Rad, the essays put together by Bernhard Anderson (editor) in his book *Creation in the Old Testament*, a recent Ph.D. dissertation (unpublished) by Brett Lamberty on "Natural Cycles in Ancient Israel's View of Reality," the two-volume work by James Gustafson in *Theocentric Ethics*, and Paul Santmire's *The Travail of Nature: The Ambiguous Ecological Promise of Christian Theology*.[7] I struggle to develop a theology of the land with the documentation of the Commission of Church and Society of the World Council of Churches, which resulted in the benchmark work of the world conference on "Faith, Science and the Future," held at the Massachusetts Institute of Technology (Cambridge, 1978), on the theme "The Just, Participatory and Sustainable Society."[8]

An integration of these exegetical and ethical works results in the following summary:[9]

1. Creation (the land) of the whole world is God's, and everything that is within it. All has quality, value, and meaning to God. All life has purpose.

2. Creation is a continuous process. It provides for all the necessities of life.

3. Creation and its miracle of life are gifts bestowed by the Creator on all life.

4. This created world and its environment are not at the disposal of humankind. Rather, humankind is a representative of God as a monarch within her or his domain, to act as a steward in governing the use of the resources of life, for all life, for the purpose of keeping the creative process alive and moving forward. Humankind has responsibility for liberation, for working for the establishment of a full justice that reflects cosmic order.

This is the world view, or paradigm, of New Testament thought. The additional emphasis in the New Testament comes at this point: In Christ, we are empowered to make all things new. The best summary of this is found in Romans:

> Do not be conformed to this world, but be transformed by the renewal of your mind, that you may prove what is the will of God, what is good and acceptable and perfect. (Rom 12:2, RSV)

In his little book *Enough Is Enough*, John Vernon Taylor reminds us of a significant dimension of Christian freedom, namely, that in Christ we are free to raise questions others fear to raise, and to dare answers that the powers and principalities of our time would consider absurd.[10] It seems to me that the focus of our project on the Theology of Land is that we live out this understanding of Christian freedom as we examine the nature of the crisis we face in rural America and the future of the land, and in suggesting new directions for the achievement of a renewed vision about our relationships to the land.

For me, the exegetical insights about Old Testament understandings of the land (creation) are foundational for the construction of a renewed theology of the land. These insights are very ancient. The land, the creation, was understood to belong to God, not us. We are not free to use the land as we wish. The land, the creation, of which farm and urban and industrial acreage is a part, belongs to God. We ought to relate to the land (not use it) in a way that guarantees justice and preserves righteousness, the right order of creation. This is what "having dominion" is all about. I observe that this is what the psalmist was trying to say in Psalm 104: ". . . and let not these foundations be shaken."

In my struggle to make theological sense, I find that my working theology of land falls into what I call "Dominion Ethics." I hope that our Old Testament scholars will help us move forward in understanding the implications of this theme. Dominion Ethics is not new. The observations of the forebearers of our faith were unquestionably wise. They understood within the context of their world view that the land (the creation) is God's, not ours. Everything has meaning for the Creator. We are not free to do with the land as we please; rather, the human responsibility is to relate to the land (not use it) as responsible stewards, as a species capable of reflection and able to express gratitude for life and for the created order of planet earth, in its galaxy, that sustains life and human history, that sustains the history of the evolution of this miraculous thing called life in all its fullness. This is what it means to be "created in God's image." The psalmist portrays, not a hierarchy in which one life form has greater value than the other, but an interdependent "common-unity," in which humanity finds itself with the endowments of responsibility.

In our search for a new land ethic, it seems to me that in consideration of the works of respected scholars in Bible and theology, we must talk about relationships and responsibilities, not freedom and rights to use the land as we see fit. Continual reference in so much of this Old Testament literature speaks of land relationships and duties to the whole community of life and its future. It speaks of the duty to replenish, restore, and preserve the land. God has enabled us, by the design of creation, to relate to the land, but not use it, as we relate to, but do not use, our families. The central theme in Dominion Ethics is, in the words of Claus Westermann in *Elements of Old Testament Theology*, to restore and preserve the land . . . the creation. [11] He goes on to say that "every form of exploitation is an expression of our human contempt of God's commission to have dominion."[12] Westermann suggests that in the time of the ancient Hebrews, whenever a king was incapable of responsible dominion, he forfeited his domain. [13] Thus, our work and relationships have to be evaluated in the light of whether they restore and preserve the resources and relationships within creation and contribute to the maintenance of a full justice and right order (an ecological concept). We are called as a human community to understand the blessings of life, not in terms of bountiful harvest, but rather as a steady flow of daily life. Worship gives reference to the preservation, strengthening, and renewal of this original blessing. "We are to relate to all things," in the words of James Gustafson in *Ethics from a Theocentric Perspective*, "as all things relate and have meaning to the creator and creation."[14] Gustafson goes on to say that "we hardly know what this really means and demands."[15] So we can see the nature of the challenge that is before us in working toward clarification about our theology of the land.

Born out of what I call, for want of a better term, Dominion Ethics is the idea of a regenerative agriculture that restores, sustains, and preserves. What a challenge this is in the context of seven thousand years of human destruction of the land! [16] What a challenge this is to our sophisticated science and technology to invent, with new biological, physical, and social tools (for the first time in human history since we all settled into permanent communities), an agricultural system that restores and preserves the elements essential for the food system!

Born out of the tradition of dominion ethics is a renewed vision with a new hope. It seems to me that in our discussions, debates, and pastoral letters, our task is to lift up this hope, vision, and ethical foundation. This ought to be the content of our advocacy about what we are hoping to see our nation achieve, and the purpose of our public policies and programs for a new agriculture born out of a time-tested land ethic. Our task is to work prophetically during this time in our national and global history (a time when political leaders have lost their way in meeting the immediate demands of their circumstances and are caught in outworn ideologies borrowed from past histories and contexts) to articulate new visions and to communicate these visions.[17] This is an awesome working agenda for those who claim discipleship in following him who called us to pursue God's kingdom of justice and righteousness. In his book *The Land*, Walter Brueggemann lifts us to a new level of understanding about the meaning of "a forgotten dimension of ministry." He points to the task of being "visionaries and question-putters" for those of power and position, of being confidants to the kings and queens and governors.[18]

III. WHAT ARE THE IMPLICATIONS OF SUCH A THEOLOGY OF THE LAND IN RELATION TO SUCH ISSUES AS LAND OWNERSHIP, LAND USE, AGRICULTURE, AND HUMAN COMMUNITY?

I have added the word "agriculture" to this original question that was set before us for consideration. I build upon it in response to the question. I do so with the feeling that we must understand agriculture and global food needs as a prerequisite perspective for proposing answers. I sense that leaving this word out of the question was a serious oversight. Let me try to demonstrate why I have this concern.

A regenerative agriculture, coherent and consistent with a tradition of what I have called Dominion Ethics, an ethic that requires our relationships to the land to be restoring and preserving, will be solar and biologically intensive. It will be labor intensive. Farmers will be understood as "managers of micro-biotic communities," of which there are millions! We will call this kind of agriculture "agro-ecology."[19] This activity is biologically very complex. It is not truncated as are today's monocropping systems. Farms and farming systems will be designed to be, in the words of Wendell Berry and others, "analogues of original ecosystems."[20] Agricultural colleges will be called "schools of agro—ecology," or "schools of biotic community management." Farming will be site-specific. It will harmonize and enhance the massive diversity of ecological niches. Zero tillage, or permaculture, will be the rule. Such an agriculture will integrate perennial grasses, trees, and indigenous animal species into the system. It will involve the unlocking of the genetic potential of more than twenty thousand identified edible plants. Today 85 percent of all food consumed by humanity comes from fourteen plants: wheat, rice, sorghum, millet, corn, barley, bananas, coconut, cassava, yams, potatoes, soybeans, peas, and table beans. An "agro-ecology" will involve the development of the food potential of more plant species as well as the ranching of indigenous animals, such as the antelope, bison, elk, cape buffalo, zebra, and giraffe. We will talk in terms of prairie farming, woodland farming, lowland farming, desert farming, tropical forest farming, sahelian farming. In livestock production we will work symbiotically with creatures that have evolved within their ecosystems for tens of thousands of years and have contributed to the health and balance of the plant communities of their natural habitats.

New agricultural infrastructures for research, food production, and processing will unfold. Agriculture will be regionalized. This is the antithesis of present developments in vertical integration and the agribusiness approaches to monocropping . . . systems of tremendous destructive force. Agro-ecology will engineer itself in ways that maintain and enhance the health of the land and those who toil upon it. Agribusiness (as we define it today) will fade just as soon as oil, gasoline, and nitrogen fertilizers skyrocket in price by the mid-1990s. Undoubtedly, large-scale, capital-intensive agricultural assets will shift to other more profitable places once artificial tax structures that now favor corporate investments in agriculture are modified to reflect a wider justice for folks still on the land. When this happens, the search will begin once again for the wisdom of memory and song of the former folk who understood the meaning of healthy relations with the land.

We have a long way to go, but the journey has already begun in many significant places. The basic values of a regenerative agriculture (responsible freedom for responsible society, meaningfulness in work and relationship, life and future) give reason and hope for a new agriculture. The guidelines of justice and regenerativeness are guidelines for value and theological construct actualization. In a regenerative agriculture, mechanistic, dualistic, and Machiavellian paradigms will shift to a new one that will be more coherent and consistent with the human purpose of coparticipation in the creative process.

For a postmodern world, farms will be analagous to original biotic communities. Farmers are to be site-specific managers of these complex and extremely fragile plant and animal communities. Rural human communities will be understood as the fundamental support structures of the farmers: technological, educational, recreational, aesthetic, economic, religious, and memory. Without quality rural communities, farmers cannot function in responsible ways. We already recognize that for a biologically and labor intensive agro-ecology to exist, perhaps 30 percent of a nation's population should be on the land, not 1 to 3 percent. This is how I think about family farms and rural community. If you dismantle them, you destroy the nation's food system and its resource base, as well as fundamental structures of social justice and the checks-and-balances system of political and economic power. I have seen too many national tragedies across the face of the globe to think otherwise. Walter Goldschmidt forcefully warned of these things long ago.[21]

Specifically, what are the implications of all this discussion? (a) There is no such thing as land ownership in human terms. The term "land use" is vulgar. To the contrary, we have to start thinking about the meaning of "relationship" to the land as "coparticipants" living out the meaning of "created in God's image." (b) Using the outline about responsible farm policy suggested in the closing sections of Neil Sampson's *Farmland or Wasteland*, there should be, first of all, a moratorium on the conversion of prime agricultural land as well as on farm foreclosures. [22] Of further immediate need in farm policy is the legislation to enable the rejuvenation of all our nation's past achievements in water, grassland, forest, and soil conservation. (c) Every effort is needed in farm policy to broaden truncated understandings about the nature and responsibility of agricultural research so that it focuses on the development of a regenerative agriculture. (d) The implications of all this are that United States agricultural production will be reduced, perhaps by 50 percent, so that it will be within the regenerative capacities of the nation's ecosystems. This will require massive shifts in the entire nation's economy. We will have to pay for what it costs to produce food on a regenerative basis, not a subsidized one based on artificial pricing of petrochemicals derived from the earth's nonrenewable resource base, food subsidized by discounting the future. In terms of implications of a new land-relation ethic, which I have called a Dominion Ethic, our foreign policy will need to give primary attention to cooperating with other nations in building within the food-deficit world "self-reliant and regenerative food systems." Thus it is that for many reasons the idea of building and maintaining a national economy, in part by earnings from the sale of agricultural commodity surplus on foreign markets, must give way to the necessities and environmental limitations of a regenerative self-reliant food system. [23] For the meeting of these needs (growing out of one's logical projection of the implications of a new land ethic that requires restoration and preservation) is the necessity to make a theological shift from the kind of narrow anthropocentrism that Lyn White Jr. so eloquently described two decades ago [24] to a genuine theocentrism. Such a shift will approximate the magnitude of the task outlined in Gustafson's *Ethics*. [25] In this shift we finally go full circle and meet the challenge laid before us many years ago when Aldo Leopold said:

> A thing is right when it contributes to the integrity, harmony and beauty of the biotic community. It is wrong when it goes the other way. [26]

Every time I reflect upon this ethic, I ask myself: "Is there anything that we do that even begins to approximate this mandate?" I also ask, "How long can the planet maintain its health if we as a human species compromise this standard?"

Finally, by way of identifying some of the many implications of a new land ethic, an ethic of relationships to the whole of creation (the land) and the future, I want to suggest, for the benefit of this critically important project, that the Catholic bishops' pastoral letter on the United States economy gives as strong a recognition as is possible to our new reality that resources are very limited, nearing exhaustion, and very fragile. We live in a new world of limits that challenges our sciences, technology, and modern life-style to help us all live up to the standard of regenerative relations with the planet's resource base.

IV. HOW OUGHT WE TO THINK ABOUT A NEW LAND ETHIC IN THE CONTEXT OF WORLD FOOD NEEDS?

First of all, we must have knowledge (memory) of what has happened in historic times if we are to be honest in confronting this question. Historically, because of human abuse of the land, 50 percent of the earth's arable soil resources have been eroded away. Given the present trend in desert encroachment as a consequence of bad agriculture everywhere in the world, the United Nations Food and Agricultural Organization and the United Nations Environmental Program predict that about 33 percent of this remaining deposit will be lost by the year 2000 (fifteen years from now). Thus by the turn of the century, when the Christian world will be pondering the nature of its mission at the beginning of its third millennium of witness and service, more than six billion people will be attempting to support themselves on a little less than 5 percent of the earth's surface. [27] It is no wonder that we talk about a moratorium on prime agricultural land and farm foreclosures! It is no wonder, in the context of this reality, that the question about food security and the security of those who produce the food crops of the nations is so critically important. We must ponder the theology of the land within this global context of loss, grinding rural poverty, and a morally, technologically, environmentally, and economically bankrupt agriculture. There is no way that we can be responsible in our theologizing without being aware of the magnitude of humanity's destructive history of the land.

Dominion Ethics as applied to the call for a new agriculture requires international effort to cooperate with food deficit nations (more than 120 nations are far outside the hopes of self-reliant, self-sufficient food systems) in the development of a self-reliant and regenerative food system. This means that we have to work very hard and without much more loss of time in undoing the last two hundred years of colonial occupation that has left the earth devastated from the legacies of unmanaged cattle rearing, and the production of such colonial crops for export to the colonial nations as cotton, peanuts, maize, sugar, pineapple, bananas, peas, coffee, spices, and pyrethrum.

A new agriculture has to address, on a regenerative basis, the conquest of rural poverty in the nations. Rural poverty is not only a testimony to massive human exploitation and injustice; it is also the seedbed of the environmentally threatening issue of stressful population densities. A new agriculture must address the need to restore climatic patterns that are now in disarray from deforestation and fire, annual cropping systems on fragile tropical soil resources, and uncontrolled cattle grazing. A new land ethic has to stand the test of universal biospheric stability. This means that we must understand security in terms of genetic diversity and predictable climatic patterns. In pondering the issues associated with the theology of the land, we must come to understand that the first priority, in the words of Nobel Prize winner René Dubos (in *Wooing the Earth*), is to rehabilitate our stressed landscapes. [28] Old Testament scholars help us to see that creation history is prior and instrumental to human history. A new theology of the land causes us to rethink our anthropocentrically oriented theology about creation and of our relationship to it.

SUMMARY

The idea of Dominion Ethics requires regenerative relationships with the land. Abusive human relations with the land (creation) now equal the threat of nuclear weaponry. The end result can be the conversion of the earth to another lifeless planet within the galaxy. Time is running short, biologically speaking, for making a massive transition to what, for want of a better term, is called a "postmodern world." Basic to this needed transition is a new theological orientation about creation and the human place within it. Basic to a needed transition is a new world view.

Responsible theology results in responsible ethics. Old Testament mainstream theology underscores the perception that the land (the creation) is God's. All aspects have meaning and purpose for God. We are not free to do with the land as we please; rather we, created in God's image, have been endowed with the responsibility for maintaining justice and righteousness within the dominion. This requires the restoration and preservation of all the resources of the domain.

Basic to all life is food. For the human species, agriculture is a basic activity involving foundational relationships with the land and all who dwell upon it. Coherent with the idea of "dominion" (in the best exegetical interpretation that can be brought to this word) is the idea of a regenerative food system . . . a regenerative pattern of our sustenance. Thus within this frame of reference, we can hope to develop new perspectives and insights about "land ownership," land use, farming, human community, rural community, life-style, agriculture (agro-ecology), farm policy, farm foreclosure, agricultural research agenda, species extinction, food as a weapon, food for the generation of national income and trade balancing mechanisms, and about soil, forest and water loss, atmospheric stress, and responsible foreign policy.

In the closing decades of the twentieth century, where humanity recognizes the collision course of its technosphere with the biosphere of its inheritance, pondering the issue of the theology of the land results in the recognition of the need to shift from a human-centeredness to a God-centeredness. In this process we gain fresh insight about our relation to the land. In the words of Paul Santmire in *The Travail of Nature*, contemporary Christian theology is "profoundly ambiguous" about so many of these fundamental relational issues.[29] The theological task before us is awesome, promising, and transforming.

1. Carl Sagan, *Cosmos* (New York: Random House, 1980). See ch. 13, "Who Speaks for the Earth?" and Rolf Knierim, "Cosmos and History in Israel's Experience."

2. Lawrence Busch, and William B. Lacy, *Science, Agriculture, and the Politics of Research* (Boulder, Colo.: Westview Press, 1983).

3. Don A. Dillman, and Daryl J. Hobbs, *Rural Society in the U.S.: Issues for the 1980's* (Boulder, Colo.: Westview Press, 1982).

4. Kenneth A. Dahlberg, *Evaluation of Agricultural Research: The Choice of Evaluative Concepts and Indicators and Their Relation to National Goals.* To be published in 1986 by Michigan State University, Kalamazoo, Mich.

5. For a good survey of the crisis, see the following works: R. Neil Sampson, *Farmland or Wasteland* (Emmaus, Penn.: Rodale, 1981); Charles Lutz, (ed.), *Farming the Lord's Land: Christian Perspectives on American Agriculture* (Minneapolis: Augsburg Publishing House, 1980); Robert Grey, (ed.), *National Agricultural Land Study: The Protection of Farmland.* (Washington, D.C.: U.S. Government Printing Office, 1981); C. Dean Freudenberger, *Food for Tomorrow?* (Minneapolis: Augsburg, 1984).

6. E. F. Schumacher, *Small is Beautiful: Economics as if People Mattered* (New York: Harper and Row, 1973).

7. H. Paul Santmire, *The Travail of Nature: The Ambiguous Ecological Promise of Christian Theology* (Philadelphia: Fortress Press, 1985).

8. See the World Council of Churches Documents, *Faith and Science in an Unjust World*, vols. I, II, and *Faith, Science and the Future* (Geneva, 1979).

9. For a full development of this issue, see Freudenberger, *Food for Tomorrow?* (Minneapolis: Augsburg Publishing House, 1984).

10. John Vernon Taylor, *Enough Is Enough* (Great Britain: SCM Press, Ltd., 1975).

11. Claus Westermann, *Elements of Old Testament Theology* (Atlanta: John Knox Press, 1983), pp. 98–99.

12. *Ibid.*, p. 98.

13. *Ibid.*

14. James Gustafson, *Ethics from a Theocentric Perspective*, vol. 1 (Chicago: University of Chicago Press, 1983), pp. 327ff.

15. *Ibid.*

16. See W.C. Lowdermilk, *The Conquest of the Land Through 7,000 Years* (Washington, D.C.: Superintendent of Documents, 1978).

17. Lester R. Brown, *The State of the World, 1985* (New York: W.W. Norton, 1985), p. 245.

18. Walter Brueggemann, *The Land* (Philadelphia: Fortress Press, 1977), p. 113.

19. William Lockeretz, (ed.), *Environmentally Sound Agriculture* (New York: Praeger, 1983).

20. Wendell Berry, *The Gift of Good Land* (San Francisco: North Point, 1981).

21. For an "early warning" statement on the perils of corporate agriculture, see Walter Goldschmidt, *As You Sow: Three Studies in the Social Consequences of Agribusiness* (Montclair: Allanheld and Sosmun, 1978).

22. R. Neil Sampson, *Farmland or Wasteland* (Emmaus, Penn.: Rodale, 1981).

23. See Freudenberger, "The Politics of Food," in *World and Word, Winter edition*, Arland Hultgren, (ed.) (St. Paul: Luther Northwestern Seminaries, 1985).

24. Lyn White, Jr., "The Religious Roots of Our Ecological Crisis." *Science*, vol. 155, no. 3767.

25. James M. Gustafson, *Ethics From a Theocentric Perspective*, vols. I and II (Chicago: University of Chicago Press, 1983, 1984).

26. Aldo Leopold, *A Sand County Almanac* (Oxford: Oxford University Press, 1966).

27. United Nations, Secretariat of the United Nations Conference on Desertification, *Desertification: Its Causes and Consequences* (New York: Pergamon, 1977).

28. René Dobos, *The Wooing of Earth* (New York: Scribner, 1981).

29. H. Paul Santmire, *The Travail of Nature: The Ambiguous Ecological Promise of Christian Theology* (Philadelphia: Fortress Press, 1985).

4

Land, Theology, and the Future

John Hart

Across the United States today, the auctioneer's gavel hammers away at farmers' homesteads and pounds into dust farmers' dreams. Economically and psychologically depressed farm families are forced off the land, into the cities, and toward an uncertain future.

Throughout the United States today, the congressional gavel hammers away at government treaties and pounds into dust their promises to Native Americans. Economically and psychologically depressed native peoples are forced off their lands, into government housing, and toward a condition of increased poverty, government dependency, and federal control.

Hovering in the background, benefiting from the results of those gavels, are a handful of individuals and corporate controllers: this wealthy elite expects to profit from the poverty of the masses of displaced peoples of the land and to exercise greater political and economic power over the land, its fruits, and its people.

CRISES AND CROSSROADS

There are several crises that confront peoples of the land today.

There is a *crisis of ownership*. The limited lands of the national domain are being gathered into fewer and fewer hands. Increasing numbers of people are being uprooted from the soil and left without a stake in land that was carefully cultivated or freely roamed by their ancestors for generations.

There is a *crisis of use*. The soil, the forest, the rivers, and the ground itself are exploited with little apparent concern for social or environmental effects. Poisoned air blows across the land, poisoned water flows through and seeps into the land, and poisoned soil blankets the land.

There is a *crisis of values*. In contrast to the best ideals of the political founders of the American republic and of the religious founders of the church communities that people that republic, *greed* has replaced *need* as the prevailing response to questions of land ownership and use.

At particular points in history social groups evaluate where they have been and where they are going as a people. They are aware of divergent possibilities of choices for their future and might see themselves at a crucial crossroads of their existence. For some time now some social analysts have been proposing that this nation is at such a point. The choice confronting us, they have said, is whether we shall walk the road that leads to care for the earth, care for one another as members of a single human family under God, and care for the other creatures of God, or whether we shall destroy the earth and all life, gradually or in an instant. At the crossroads there diverge the way of life and the way of death.

For several years I have used such images. But after traveling across the country, meeting with diverse peoples, assessing events reported in the media, and reflecting on where we are going as a nation, I have reached a more pessimistic evaluation. It seems to me that as a nation, we have passed the crossroads and have chosen death rather than life. Despite the pleas of those who love the earth, despoilation of the environment increases. Despite the cries of farmers and native peoples, displacement from the land increases. Despite the petitions of peacemakers, preparation for the ultimate war increases. So it is not now a matter of considering two paths before us; rather, a more difficult task confronts us:

that of turning back from the way that we walk, finding again that crucial turning point, and redirecting our steps and our energies toward harmony with our earth, our God, and each other as children of God and of the earth.

GREED, NEED, AND CREED

There are three major attitudes dominating the relations that people have with their land today. These attitudes emanate from the operative ideology of those working the land, either for themselves or for others.

For some, unrestrained *greed* underlies their relations with the land. For such people, acquisition of land or of the wealth that accrues from the land's products is of paramount importance. Land is seen as matter to be exploited—as much and as quickly as possible—in order to satisfy the wants of the exploiter. Within this perspective the rights to own land and to determine its use are dependent upon financial status. Those who have the most money in a given situation have the right to outbid others for ownership of land and/or determination of its use.

The attitude of greed is primarily an *atheistic* and *antisocial* perspective: God's ultimate dominion is unacknowledged, and the owner's wants are voraciously pursued at the expense of the pressing needs of other members of the human family. Thus a farmer might add "field to field" (see Isa 5:8), plow from fence row to fence row, and pile chemical upon chemical in order to increase a bank account and plunge more fully into the "frenzy of consumerism" (see Pope John Paul II, *Homily in Yankee Stadium*, New York, October 2, 1979). Or members of an Indian tribal council— an organization imposed upon native peoples by the United States government, and answerable ultimately to the federal government and not to those governed—might sign oil, coal, gas, or uranium leases with an energy corporation so that council members might retain their pre-eminent financial and political positions within their ethnic nation.

For others, pressing *need* governs their quest for land and their designation of its use. In this case individual or family considerations and, in the ideal situation, the needs of the broader human community and even of the land itself determine the extent of acquisitions and the manner in which such acquisitions are used. Sometimes in situations of economic crisis—such as the present moment—short-term individual or family needs might take precedence over long-term land needs.

This is primarily an *agnostic* and *asocial* perspective: the realization of one's responsibilities to God and to humanity occasionally intervenes in land practices, but the pressing needs of the moment override consideration of these responsibilities. For example, a farmer caught in a cost/price squeeze and in danger of losing a family homestead might, in the hope of retaining the land for future family use, wager present exploitation of the soil against the possibility that the soil might become so depleted that the land would be useless for agriculture in the future. Or members of an Indian tribal council, anguished by the poverty of their reservation, might sell or lease energy-rich sections of the reservation in the present, even though that might mean a further diminished land base from which members of the community might derive their livelihood in the future.

Finally, a particular religious *creed* might permeate the ways in which people relate to the land. For some, there might be a consciousness that the earth is the Lord's, and that people are stewards of God's earth. Others might acknowledge the presence of the Creator and their responsibilities toward the Creator, but also see the earth itself as sacred, as a mother-provider giving life to her children. The result of these perspectives is that people respect and care for the earth and seek to relate to it in such a way that it will renew itself and continue to provide for the needs of those who depend on it for their lives and livelihoods.

As a consequence, people holding this perspective see the earth as a *sacred trust:* it is held *from* the Creator and *for* all life, now and into the ages to come. This perspective, then, is primarily *theistic* and *social*. So farmers considering a land purchase might ask themselves if they truly need new acreage for themselves or their children, or if they should support a young aspiring farm family's effort to enter into agriculture as an independent owner/operator. Or the traditional elders of an Indian nation might resist the allotment of communal reservation lands into individual parcels that would be sold off in times of economic hardship or need, and so retain their people's lands for their people. And within both groups, the sovereignty of the Creator would be recognized, and reverence for lands entrusted by the Creator would be practiced.

The three bases of land relations—greed, need, and creed—are all encountered in the United States today. However, the dominant land ethic—if indeed the term "ethic" can be used—is that of *greed.* Its effects can be seen in the consolidation of the land into fewer hands and in the exploitation of the land with fewer benefits and fewer benefiting.

As we consider the present situation, two basic questions arise that demand a response: (1) Who should own the land? and (2) How should the land be used? According to the prevailing "wisdom," the land should be owned by the one(s) having the wherewithal to purchase it when it becomes available, no matter whether need or greed prompts their efforts at land acquisition. And it should be used in whatever manner that owner decides is most beneficial—that is, most profitable—no matter what the environmental (land) impacts or social (people) impacts of that use. In contrast to this attitude stand the insights of religious faith: Yahweh, not Mammon and not Mars, is the God to be served.

RELIGIOUS REFLECTIONS

A careful analysis of the Christian and Native American traditions reveals that for people of faith, a basic contradiction exists between the prevailing profit ideology that elevates greed to a virtue and religious teachings that relegate greed to a vice and propose stewardship and sharing as virtues.

I would like to share with you some reflections based on the Scriptures in particular and the Christian tradition in general. (These ideas are developed more fully in my book *The Spirit of the Earth.*)

For the Christian, three basic principles should permeate questions of land ownership and use:

1. The earth is God's (by creation: Gen 1, Ps 8:2-5; 24:1; by statement: Lev 25:23);

2. The earth is entrusted by God to humanity (Gen 2); and

3. The earth and her fruits are to be shared equitably through the ages (Jubilee Year: Lev 25:8-55; Isa 61:1-2; Luke 4:17-21; judgment on the basis of the distribution of the earth's fruits: Matt 25:31-46).

These Christian principles parallel and in part become congruent with principles that might be deduced from the traditions of indigenous peoples of the Americas. Such principles would be:

1. Mother Earth is sacred and cannot be owned;

2. Mother Earth is to be respected and cared for; and

3. Mother Earth's gifts are to be shared by all living beings through the ages.

MOTHER EARTH AND OUR RELATIVES

For native peoples the earth is a sacred mother-provider. Her extent is to be open to the whole community, without unnatural barriers (such as fences) dividing people. As mother, she cannot be owned—people do not own a parent.

Mother Earth, who gives life to all creatures, deserves their respect. And if she is to continue providing for them in the future, her fruits must be gathered according to need and accepted with gratitude, and her productive capacity cared for.

In the native perspective, a certain equality exists among all living beings populating Mother Earth. Humanity is not seen as superior to other life forms; all life is interrelated and worthy of respect. This consciousness of respect for life in its many manifestations is very evident in the words with which many native people begin and end their ceremonies: "All my relatives." The designation "my relatives" is not limited to people; it refers to the four-legged, the winged, the finned, the rooted, and the two-legged forms of life. All have worth in the eyes of the Creator; all are children of Mother Earth.

In native cultures religion and daily life cannot be separated. Religious practices are not just one part of a culture: they are expressions of the culture, while the culture itself flows from religious belief.

During the past six years I have come to know, respect, and befriend spiritual and political leaders from several native nations of the area of God's earth now called the United States of America by cartographers and politicians (among others who artificially divide up this one world and separate members of the human family from each other). I would like to share some insights that they have shared with me. What I pass on to you has been passed on to me, for the most part orally, in much the same way that these traditions have been transmitted for centuries among native peoples (and also, as we know, how the Old Testament/Hebrew Scriptures began, and how Jesus taught in the formative years of Christianity).

This past summer I traveled to Arizona, Oklahoma, and northern New York to visit with and learn from traditional native peoples. Among them were traditional elders, such as the Hopi Thomas Banyacya; traditional chiefs, such as Leon Shenandoah, of the Onondaga nation; and a great Muskogee-Creek medicine man and spiritual leader, Phillip Deere. I found that these people shared a common belief in the Creator, respect for Mother Earth, belief in the interrelatedness of all creatures, a sense of pride and sovereignty, and an activist commitment to social justice.

Conflict at Big Mountain

In an area of Arizona known as the Black Mesa, a confrontation has been brewing that threatens to boil over into armed conflict between traditional Navajos—whose ancient name is Diné ("the people")—and Hopi tribal police supported by federal troops. The conflict concerns land use, land rights, native sovereignty, and religious and cultural freedom. The United States government intends to force the relocation, by July 8, 1986, of some ten to fourteen thousand Diné from lands upon which they have herded sheep for centuries.

The reasons for the forced relocation are basically two: a few Hopi cattle ranchers want more pasture land for their herds, and a few giant energy corporations—paramount among them Peabody Coal—want more lands for coal strip-mining or oil, gas, and uranium extraction. The desire for wealth of a few—those who seek to satisfy *wants*—are taking precedence over the hope for a continued land base on the part of the many—those who seek to satisfy *needs*.

Evident in the comments of Diné people who are resisting displacement, and of their traditional Hopi allies, is their perspective on the land and the roots of that perspective in their religious faith.

When questioned about her resistance to relocation, Pauline Whitesinger (who speaks no English) noted that "in our traditional tongue there is no word for relocation. To move away means to disappear and never be seen again." Other Diné members have declared that the word for "move away" means "to die." These statements reveal the strong attachment traditional peoples feel for place, for the land on which they were born, grew up, work, and expect to die, in which they expect to be buried, and of which they will then become a part of Mother Earth's efforts to care for her children when their bodies decay and provide nourishment for others of her life forms.

I interviewed Pauline Whitesinger in June (1985) when she was attending a meeting between traditional Diné and Hopi in the Hopi village Hotevilla. She expressed to me, through an interpreter, her strong resolve to continue fighting for her land and her religious values: "I have no place to go. The only way that I will leave is if I die, if they kill me, or if I die there naturally. My spirit will remain there on my land when I die."

For Pauline, the land "was given to us (the Diné) by the Creator," and cannot be taken away by anyone else. And, "there is a strong tie between us and the land. Otherwise, we would be like birds flying in the air, or like fish swimming in the water."

Even though "the land was put here for native people to use" by none other than the Creator, "The white man saw it, and now he wants to take it away from us." Ties with this gift from the Creator are strong and should not be severed: "There is no place like mine. I was born on that land, and it is where my umbilical cord is buried. It is where my roots are."

The Diné people are supported by traditional Hopi people, who oppose the actions of the Hopi tribal council that is dominated by Mormon Hopis. Traditional Hopis refuse to take part in the council, seeing it as a white-imposed institution that is subversive of the ancient religious-based system of elders' leadership of the people. For Fermina Banyacya, a woman elder from Kykotsmovi on Third Mesa, the relocation effort represents an ongoing white attitude toward native peoples:

> When Christopher Columbus came, he thought that he had discovered a new world; but native people were already here. He and other white people thought that we just went with the land, that we were savages or animals and couldn't think. But this was and is our land: it belonged and belongs to the Hopi and other native people. We have always had our land and our form of government. The United States government has tried to make us their wards and set up tribal governments, but we have never signed any treaty nor given them any land. We will never accept their government; we have our traditional government. The "Tribal Council" is only a puppet government of the BIA [Bureau of Indian Affairs] and the United States government; anything that it decides has to be approved by the United States government. We are an independent people and cannot accept that.

The Hopi Prophecies

In 1947 a Hopi elder called together members of several Hopi clans to share with them an ancient vision of his clan, a vision that dated from a time before the arrival of the first white immigrants. The prophecy was that a gourd of ashes would fall from the sky, and that where the ashes landed, nothing would grow. The elder believed that the prophecy referred to the atomic bomb (which was first dropped on American Indian land, then twice on Japan). Other clan members then shared their own clan prophecies. The Hopi concluded that the world was entering a period of crisis in which great catastrophe would result if political practices did not change, and if mistreatment of the earth and her peoples continued.

Among the prophecies made public thus far are predictions of a group of people who would dress in different ways, have their own life-style, and have a name similar to "Hopi" ("Hippies" went to the Hopi lands in the mid-sixties); that there would be a "road into the sky" (airport runways are believed to fulfill that vision); that the earth would be shaken three times by major wars (World Wars I and II are seen as partial fulfillments; at Hopi dances a gourd symbolizing the world is shaken to remind the people to be watchful); that two Purifiers would come from the east to bring justice to the earth and her peoples; and that if the latter did not fulfill their responsibilities, a crueler Purifier would come from the west. Hopi spiritual leaders have tried unsuccessfully on two occasions to address the United Nations about their prophecies. They are supposed to make one more effort to do so, in order that the world might change.

The Hopi religion and prophecies reveal this people's deep concern for the well-being of the earth, and their recognition that they—and we—are dependent on the earth for our own well-being.

Lacrosse and Liberation

Just south of Syracuse, New York, lies the land of the Onondaga nation. The Onondaga are one of the member groups of the old Six Nations confederacy (Onondaga, Mohawk, Cayuga, Seneca, Oneida, and Tuscarora). An Onondaga chief, Leon Shenandoah, is also *Thadodahho*—chief of chiefs—of all six nations.

Members of the confederacy have prophecies with themes similar to those of the Hopi. In fact, when the Hopi first decided to try to teach the world to change, they went to the Onondaga to share insights. Six Nations prophecies—many dating to Handsome Lake, who revealed them in the early nineteenth century—describe the dissolution of the white society and the devastation of this country. Leon

Shenandoah believes that the time for their fulfillment is approaching. He states that although the United States Constitution is based in part on traditional Six Nations government (Thomas Jefferson and Benjamin Franklin were familiar with this governing process, part of which is seen in the division of the three powers—executive, legislative, and judicial—and in committee workings), the United States cannot survive as a nation: "They took our government but left out our spirituality." That spirituality included a sense of justice and sharing, and a great respect for Mother Earth. When speaking with me, Leon held up a dollar bill and said, "This is spirituality for them."

Sovereignty is an important issue on the Onondaga reservation. Onondaga members travel on their own passports when going overseas, and are recognized as representatives of a political entity having no official diplomatic exchange with the countries they visit. The Onondaga nation is negotiating with Great Britain now over the possibility of a series of lacrosse games with British lacrosse teams. The playing of even one game would represent, for the Onondaga, an implicit recognition of their sovereignty by Great Britain—and a small step toward their ultimate liberation from domination by the governments of the United States and New York State (governments whose jurisdiction the Onondaga do not recognize).

Phillip Deere

One of the great personal experiences of my life was the opportunity to become friends with and share in the spiritual insights of Phillip Deere, a Muskogee-Creek spiritual leader and medicine man from Okemah, Oklahoma. Phillip was an extraordinary human being: a man of deep spiritual convictions, recognized as a spiritual leader both by fundamentalist Creek Christians (he had been a Baptist preacher for twenty years) and by traditional Muskogee people (he had been a traditional leader and healer for most of his life—including his years as a preacher). He was internationally recognized as a spokesperson for American Indian religion and the native struggle for justice. Phillip died of cancer one month ago (August 1985) at the age of fifty-nine. I feel a great sense of loss because our dialogues have ended. But I am yet conscious of his presence, and asked for his guidance in writing this article.

Phillip Deere had an extraordinary memory and a wealth of information about the history, struggles, and traditions of his people. He was a man full of compassion; he projected as well a great spiritual presence. I would like to share with you some of his insights, thoughts that he shared with me over the years.

Green Corn and Renewal

"The corn was the main food of our people, and every year there was a ceremony for the corn. No one was allowed to eat fresh corn until the ceremonies were over. During this big event, one year ended and the next one began for our people. So at the end of this year, during the green corn ceremonies, a lot of old things were renewed. In ancient times even dishes, even clothes were destroyed. New clothing was made and worn at this time. A new fire was built at the center of the circle. They renewed the fire, they renewed everything; they cleansed their grounds out, and they renewed themselves by cleansing themselves in the ceremonies. A new life began with our people. The old grudges, the old disagreements were all forgiven to one another, and everybody was at peace to start a new life.

"In ancient times when one committed wrong or committed a crime, their lives were not taken. They were spared, and sometimes they were banished from their villages to live in the mountains. And if someone survived, and if he lived alone in the wilderness up until the green corn ceremony, his crimes were all forgiven. Life started over with our people during the green corn ceremonies."

Communal Sharing

"Our kind of life continued to go on for thousands of years. The ceremonial grounds that we had were communities.

People lived a communal type of living, having their own streets, having their own homes, having their own little spots for gardening in the fields; but they also had the nation's gardens, the nation's fields, where everybody came and worked together and stored food. They had the nation's storehouse in which they stored corn. In case of a crop failure for some family, they were welcome to use the corn out of the nation's corncrib. And so people took care of one another in this communal type of living."

The attitude of sharing described by Phillip was characteristic of the native peoples in North America. In the practice of communal life Phillip described, the Christian can easily find parallels with the description of the Christian community found in the Book of Acts: "The company of those who believed were of one heart and soul, and no one said that any of the things which he possessed was his own . . ." (See 2:42-47; 4:32-37). Tragically, the sharing perspective of native peoples and of the Bible were absent from the attitudes of the majority of the white immigrants and their descendants—even though it was present in their Sacred Scriptures!

Plants and People

"At one time, in the early days of the creation, we were told . . . that the human beings had no friends and could have been destroyed by huge animals, large animals that were giants that walked upon this earth at one time. There was sickness coming upon the people with no cure whatsoever. And finally the herbs spoke out and said, " 'We, too, are trampled down; we, too, are wounded at times by these animals and by these bugs and insects. We will be your friends. We will help you.' And so this is how every herb became useful to us."

For Phillip, as with all medicine men and women, a special relationship exists between plant life and human life, as exemplified in the tale just narrated. A bond ties the two together: the concept of "higher" and "lower" life forms is absent.

Spiritual Destitution Means World Destruction

"It gives a person a feeling; it scares a person; it's frightening to see people sit around in a conference trying to figure out what they are going to do. With all the nuclear weapons that are being stored away, what are we going to do with the government? What are we going to do with the world leaders of today? How will they be able to save their countries if they have forgotten the natural laws of the human race? There will be no way that they will be able to save their countries, no matter how many conferences are held, no matter how much they assemble in the United Nations. They, too, will go west, to the setting of the sun.

"I feel that we have to get back to understanding what it is to be a human being, what it is to share and to love one another. There is no other way to eliminate the wars that go on today."

For Phillip, part of what it means to "be a human being" is to have a consciousness of one's relation to all of creation and to the Great Mystery, the One who brought creation into being and sustains it.

Creation-Focused Spirituality

"We have felt ourselves to be a part of creation: not superiors, not the rulers of creation, but only part of creation. Even our little children's stories—their bedtime stories—tell us how to respect the creation. We felt that we destroyed ourselves whenever we destroyed anything within the creation.

"Native religion to us is a way of life. That religion is based upon this creation and its sacredness. In this religion every day was a sacred day to us. Religion did not take place just Saturdays or Sundays. Every day of our life was a holy day.

"We are the caretakers of this land, and we are part of this creation. So we must respect Mother Earth. We must learn to say 'Mother' as well as we say 'Our Father.' When we destroy the creation, we destroy ourselves."

Spirituality for native peoples is creation-focused; that is, there is a strong link, a deep sense of relationship, to the created world. Any concept of human superiority to, or domination over, the rest of creation is foreign and repugnant to native peoples. People are entrusted with the role of being caretakers of *the creation of which they themselves are a part.* And, for native peoples, respect for the Creator as "Father" must be accompanied by respect for the earth as "Mother." When the earth is regarded as sacred in this way, she will be cared for, and her care of humanity will be acknowledged.

A year before he died, Phillip Deere, who had struggled so hard for justice for his people and respect for the earth, told participants at the Tenth International Indian Treaty Conference, "When I die, I will live on in the struggles of our people." In words and attitude similar to that of El Salvador's martyr Archbishop Oscar Romero, Phillip united himself in spirit to those who would carry on his mission of justice and abiding spirituality.

Hope for the Future

We have reflected on the land crisis of our time; we have seen some basic principles of land relations; and we have shared insights from the traditions of native peoples. Given the disparity between our shared values and vision and the current profit ideology, with its impacts on the earth, and given the traditional peoples' prophecies, we might ask, "Is there any hope for the future?" or even perhaps, "Is there any hope for *a* future?"

I have indicated that we have passed the crossroads. I would suggest that with an affirmation of our responsibilities toward God, each other, and the earth, and a consequent restructuring of the economic system, present political priorities, and current land practices, we might turn back to that crossroads and choose life—life for ourselves, for our children, and for our planet.

If we acknowledge our Creator and are to fulfill our responsibilities to care for our Creator's earth, we must effect some dramatic changes in American attitudes and actions. Change is possible, and the best hope for change in the current American scene is advocacy of justice by the churches. Church leaders and members in general must speak out for social change, and, through educational efforts and coalitions with groups able to work together on specific issues, create a better future for the generations that follow us. The Catholic bishops have taken a giant step toward positive social change with their pastorals on peace and economics, and in their regional statements *This Land is Home to Me* and *Strangers and Guests*. They are to be commended and encouraged to raise their prophetic voices more strongly yet.

Land Reform

There must be a fundamental reform on the land. Land must be redistributed in such a way that ownership is as broadly distributed as possible, through either moderate-sized holdings or communal holdings. Land must be used in such a way that it is carefully conserved and restored so that the earth might regenerate herself and care for future generations of the life forms that depend on her.

Steps that might be taken to achieve these goals include:

- meaningful income tax reform designed, first, to benefit the poorest among us, with disincentives to the wealthy to invest in agriculture.
- a progressive land tax that would promote moderate-sized family holdings and force the redistribution of large holdings.
- a requirement that landowners in agriculture must derive a majority of their income from agriculture.
- assistance to aspiring farmers, such as through low-interest loans.
- assistance to struggling farmers.
- exclusion of foreign ownership of land.
- protection of national forests, parks, seashores, wilderness areas, etc., as our common inheritance and as signs of respect for the earth's pristine beauty and the Creator's handiwork.
- public ownership of energy resources—oil, gas, coal, uranium—which are intended by the Creator for *responsible use* by the many, and not for *irresponsible abuse* by the few.

- workers' shares in the ownership of private industrial enterprise.
- recognition of the sovereignty of native peoples and an equitable resolution of their treaty claims.
- a shift from chemical-dependent to organic agriculture to the greatest extent feasible and as rapidly as possible.
- agricultural prices as close to parity as possible.

Religious

Reverence for God and recognition of our responsibilities before God and to each other should be demonstrated through land-related liturgies or paraliturgical practices:

- dedication of land to God when it is purchased or inherited, and annually when the seed is sown in it or new livestock brought upon it.
- offering the first fruits of the harvest to God through prayers and distribution of food to the hungry.
- periodic homiletic reminders to church congregations that they are worshiping God in God's world, a world entrusted to their care.
- an annual "Land Stewardship Sunday" throughout the United States to remind Christians that they are caretakers of God's land.
- an ecumenical attitude toward spiritual leaders of native peoples and the development of liturgies with them;
- respect for ancient religions and an openness to learning from them.

In the Old Testament/Hebrew Scriptures, we find the prophets' message of conversion and repentance, a message coupled with a warning of God's punishment if the people continue in their God-denying and people-denying ways. The prophets bring hope as well: if the people change, God will be a merciful God; and even if they do not change, God will save a remnant for the future of the nation.

As we look at the earth around us and listen to the prophets among us, we realize that we, too, are called to conversion. Our hope for a better future will be realized only to the extent that we work to make that vision the new reality. Without our engagement and immersion in the difficult struggle to create a better world—to re-create God's world—we will never find again that important crossroads we passed some time ago. And not to find it and enter the way of life is to perish.

We need a new Jubilee Year in these United States and throughout God's world. Let us begin the task of redirecting this nation away from the highway to death and to that other road of life. Let us envision and create a new and better future: for our earth, for our children, and for all life— for all generations to come. Greetings, all my relatives.

5

Rights for Life: Rebuilding Human Relationships with Land*

Richard Cartwright Austin

The Bible affirms the Lord's promise to lead us, with all creation, from slavery to freedom. "When Christ freed us, he meant us to remain free," Paul stated. "Stand firm, therefore, and do not submit again to the yoke of slavery."[1] Paul also announced that "the whole creation is eagerly waiting . . . to enjoy the same freedom and glory as the children of God."[2] Freedom implies release from oppression, whether it be slavery to an enraged Pharaoh or the affliction of disordered desires. But in the Bible freedom does not mean isolation. We are freed for relationships. We are freed for justice and compassion. We are freed to nourish and protect one another.

My concern is rebuilding human relationships with the land. In the Bible I find a moral ecology—a vision of beautiful relationships between nature, humanity, and the Lord.

*The author is grateful to John Knox Press for permission to publish ideas in this essay that are drawn from the series "Environmental Theology" to be published in 1987.

This biblical ecology involves the rescue of both humanity and the land from oppression. I will show how these relationships are expressed in the Sabbath tradition. I will then apply this biblical vision to the problem of rebuilding human relationships with land in America today. In applying the biblical ecology, I make three proposals using characteristic American language of rights and opportunities. I propose a human right of access to nature. I propose re-opening the frontier so those who wish may obtain land. And I propose rights for life, extending constitutional protection to all species of life and the systems that sustain life.

I do not limit my vision to what is possible during a Reagan administration. I try to think about what is right and what may be possible in the long term.

The Sabbath and Biblical Ecology

In the biblical tradition the Sabbath was more than a day of compulsory worship. It was a central institution of Hebrew religion, providing a framework for expressing ethical relationships between God, humanity, and nature. That is why, in Gen 1, the creation of the world was portrayed as a week ending with a Sabbath. This observance trained people in just social and ecological relationships. Through the Sabbath tradition the Hebrews discovered design in the relations between the Lord and the world, between humanity and nature, and within human society. This design became an inspired architecture for justice, a biblical ecology.

One short passage of Sabbath law illustrates how these features intertwined.

> For six years you may sow your land and gather its produce, but in the seventh year you must let it lie fallow and forego all produce from it. Those of your people who are poor may take food from it, and let the wild animals feed on what they leave. You shall do the same with your vineyard and your olive grove.

> For six days you shall do your work, but stop on the seventh day, so that your ox and your donkey may rest and the son of your slave girl have a breathing space, and the stranger too. [3]

In this example we see how the Sabbath law was used to forestall the temptation to turn work into perpetual drudgery. It gave rights to servants, children, and strangers. It provided rest for domestic animals. It gave the land fallow time for renewal. It provided the landless poor with some access to food. It even upheld a place for wild animals within the agricultural domain.

The Sabbath law dealt with freedom from inward compulsion and outward oppression, particularly those expressions most tempting in a landed society. It was an antidote to the farmer's anxiety that drives him to work perpetually.

The Sabbath law required the freeing of slaves: "When you buy a Hebrew slave, he shall serve six years, and in the seventh year he shall go out free, for nothing."[4] And these principles of restraint were applied to control greed at harvest time.

> When you reap the harvest of your land, you shall not reap right into the edges of your field; neither shall you glean the loose ears of your crop; you shall not completely strip your vineyard nor glean the fallen grapes. You shall leave them for the poor and the alien. I am the Lord your God.[5]

God's creation of the world was itself interpreted within the context of this Sabbath understanding. The authors of Genesis understood the cycle of creative energy: work was not complete until there was rest, reflection, worship, and celebration. Surely God also would wish to contemplate with joy the fruit of such awesome, primal creativity.

As God's creative days are recounted, the story conveys the Lord's delight in the vast diversity and particularity of created beings. "The earth yielded fresh growth, plants bearing seed according to their kind and trees bearing fruit each with seed according to its kind; and God saw that it was good." On the fifth day God created multitudes of birds to "fly above the earth across the vault of heaven," as well as fish and sea monsters to "swarm in the waters." God addressed them directly: the Lord's first commandment was spoken to fish and birds. "Be fruitful and increase, fill the waters of the seas; and let the birds increase on land."[6] Here, as elsewhere in the Bible, it is assumed that God can communicate with all creatures. All creatures have the capacity to receive from God and respond to God.

When men and women were created along with animals on the sixth day, we were given a special role expressed in the "image of God." In Christian and Western traditions we have spiritualized this notion of "image of God" and applied it to several human characteristics. But biblically, the image of God refers particularly to the human relationship with the land and living things. It expresses the human role to govern nature as God's representatives, to tend and keep the earth, to remember and express God's delight in all creation. Men and women are to work hard with the land, plants, and animals. Then on the Sabbath we are to join all creatures in rest, celebration, and praise to the Lord.

Humans lose the image of God when we abandon a faithful relationship with the Lord, whose servants and agents we were created to be. However, we also lose the image of God if we forsake empathetic contact with the land and our fellow creatures, which we have been deputized to cultivate and protect. To be fully human we must live in communion with both God and nature.

Sabbath law development reached a climax in the "Holiness Code" of Lev 19–26. The section has the characteristic refrain "Ye shall be holy: for I the Lord your God am holy."[7] This priestly code developed Sabbath law into a constitution of civil and ecological rights. While much of this law may never have been enforced, it was a sophisticated moral scheme to constrain human greed in an agricultural society and to give legal rights both to the landless and to the land itself.

The land was recognized to have its own rights and duties before the Lord. Like humans, it must rest periodically.

> In the seventh year the land shall keep a sabbath of sacred rest, a sabbath to the Lord. You shall not sow your field nor prune your vineyard. You shall not harvest the crop that grows from fallen grain, nor gather in the grapes from the unpruned vines.[8]

Observing that such practices were not in fact followed,

and that the land suffered in consequence, the priests were moved to prophesy that the Lord would enforce the land's rights at the expense of his people, who were not bearing the image of God to creation.

> I will scatter you among the heathen, and I will pursue you with the naked sword; your land shall be desolate and your cities heaps of rubble. Then, all the time that it lies desolate, while you are in exile in the land of your enemies, your land shall enjoy its sabbaths to the full. All the time of its desolation it shall have the sabbath rest which it did not have when you lived there.[9]

Sabbath law was also used to limit property rights and to provide for the redistribution of wealth. The principle was that the earth is the Lord's, and therefore all human ownership is relative and temporary: "No land shall be sold outright, because the land is mine, and you are coming into it as aliens and settlers."[10] Based on this principle, the Holiness Code required that debts and indentures be canceled in the seventh year. And in the fiftieth year, after seven cycles of seven, the Holiness Code proscribed a time to reverse the amassing of property by the few and to redistribute the land to the equity of the original settlement. "In this year of jubilee you shall return, every one of you, to his patrimony."[11]

While there is no evidence that such wholesale, systematic redistribution was ever accomplished in Israel, there is evidence that the validity of the principle was recognized. The injunction "Remove not the ancient landmark which your fathers have set"[12] was intended to protect these rights of redemption. There is record of one instance of redistribution after a remnant returned from the Babylonian captivity and attempted to reestablish a faithful society around Jerusalem. Their leader, Nehemiah, inveighed against the wealthy who loaned money at interest and required the pledge of debtors' children and land in collateral. He claims to have shamed the "nobles and officials" into cancelling such loans and returning all seized persons, property, and land.[13]

However Sabbath laws were enforced, they became part of the conscience of Israel, part of the moral fiber of a people attempting to live faithfully with land and with each other. Yet it would always be tempting to evade such restrictions. The prophet Amos called on the land itself to erupt beneath those who lusted to avoid Sabbath responsibilities.

> Listen to this, you who grind the destitute and plunder the humble, you who say, 'When will the new moon be over so that we may sell corn? When will the sabbath be past so that we may open our wheat again, giving short measure in the bushel and taking overweight in the silver, tilting the scales fraudulently, and selling the dust of the wheat; that we may buy the poor for silver and the destitute for a pair of shoes? The Lord has sworn by the pride of Jacob: I will never forget any of their doings.
>
> Shall not the earth shake for this? Shall not all who live on it grieve?[14]

By contrast, the virtuous Job climaxed his defense to his friends by reminding them that he had treated his land justly, as he would treat his laborers and suppliers.

> If my land has cried out in reproach at me, and its furrows have joined in weeping, if I have eaten its produce without payment and have disappointed my creditors, may thistles spring up instead of wheat, and weeds instead of barley![15]

In the Hebrew ecology the land was an active participant in a dialogue of justice, along with God and humanity. The land was hardened by abuse, but it would respond fruitfully to human care. Indeed, the land was sensitive, not just to treatment it received, but also to the quality of relationships among people and between people and God. Where people oppressed each other, they would soon afflict the land as well. Afflicted land would retaliate. "You shall therefore keep all my statutes and all my ordinances, and do them; that the land where I am bringing you to dwell may not vomit you out."[16] On the other hand, when the parties were faithful, the relationships between people, land, and God could be truly beautiful.

> Love and fidelity have come together;
> justice and peace join hands.

Fidelity springs up from earth and justice looks down from
heaven.
The Lord will add prosperity,
and our land shall yield its harvest. [17]

This distinctive ethical perspective derived from the circumstances of the Hebrew conquest of Canaan. There is a
body of scholarly opinion that Israel was formed by a rela-
tively small group who invaded from the desert and fomented
revolts among landless peasants against oppressive Canaanite
city-kings, overthrowing many of the cities of Palestine from
within. According to this theory, the trumpet that breached
the walls of Jericho was the call for freedom. The invaders
brought with them a novel faith in a Lord who set men and
women free. This faith, Walter Brueggemann suggests, became "a weapon against a hierarchal denial of land and . . .
an alternative way of understanding, distributing, and
managing land." [18]

Certainly Israel associated human freedom with living
on land of one's own, and with sensitivity to that land in obe-
dience to the Lord. "If you walk in my statutes . . . the land
shall yield its increase . . . I have broken the bars of your
yoke and made you walk erect." [19]

A Human Right of Access to Nature

For the first time in history, we have developed in the West
a society where the majority of men and women do not live
and work in direct contact with the land, the sea, or the species of natural life. We are becoming an urban culture. Even
in the Third World there is a strong trend in this direction.
We are also becoming more *humanocentric:* everything that
forms our sense of self and place and culture may now be
a human construction. The raw materials that nature provides are distant. We have pets, and we use natural materials for landscaping and decoration. But urban people need
not engage with nature seriously.

Fewer people till the land, cut the forests, mine the miner-
als, or fish the seas. Does the earth benefit from this reduced
human presence? Not at all. We burden the earth even more

than before. We lumber, farm, mine, and fish with bigger machines and more potent chemicals. Those who engage with the earth are trained, not to live with nature, but simply to harvest from it. *Agriculture*, which involved complex traditions of living in productive harmony with land, has been replaced by *agribusiness*, which is single-minded exploitation of the earth for profit. As society leaves the earth to machines, and the few people remaining are trained to think like machines, the earth suffers.

People suffer as well. Humanity suffers from a loss of awareness of God, and a loss of communion with nature. Both these capacities diminish as we are so surrounded by other people—by human constructions, ideas, and institutions—that our sense of a reality beyond the human dims. In the late 1960s some people discovered that "God is dead," while others discovered that "Nature is dying." Neither was quite true. God lives, and nature—while threatened—is still resilient. It is human culture that is sick unto death from too much fascination with power, violence, technology, and control.

John Muir was one of America's first environmental leaders. A century ago he perceived that our technological society would destroy nature if patterns of exploitation were not reversed. Muir proposed two strategies: one was to establish national parks, forests, and wilderness areas so some places might be protected from human damage or be managed more responsibly; the other was to bring people back into contact with nature. He even proposed "compulsory recreation."

> The hall and the theater and the church have been invented, and compulsory education. Why not add compulsory recreation? . . . Our forefathers forged chains of duty and habit, which bind us notwithstanding our boasted freedom, and we ourselves in desperation add link to link, groaning and making medicinal laws for relief. Yet few think of pure rest or of the healing power of Nature.[20]

Muir experienced nature as a joy in itself and an antidote to the problems of human culture. He believed people needed contact with nature to retain perspective. "Winter blows the fog out of our heads. Nature is not a mirror for the moods of the mind."[21] Muir also knew that urban Americans would not retain contact with nature unless the need to do so was clear and the opportunities to do so were apparent. Furthermore, he understood that if we lost personal contact with nature, we would lose interest in protecting it. Hence his notion of "compulsory recreation." It would be in society's interest to insure that people do, in fact, develop and maintain contact with the natural world.

Instead of "compulsory recreation" I propose *a human right of access to nature*. Every human being has the right not to be confined within the boundaries of human culture. We protect the human right of access to God with the First Amendment and a social tradition that each of us may worship God without interference. Now, in our predominantly urban culture, we also need deliberate protection of human access to nature. By law we give the physically handicapped special education and facilities so they might discover and express their human potential. We need to acknowledge that the growing class of *environmentally deprived* Americans may also need special assistance to open and maintain contact with the natural world.

The image of God in the biblical understanding implies a human vocation to express to nature, by our care of it, the justice and love of God. The biblical ecology gives humanity a key role: we are to tend and keep the earth with such faithfulness that all creation may be inspired to praise the Lord. "The whole creation is eagerly waiting . . . for the children of God."[22]

If we lose contact with God, we lose touch with the source of our life and with the beauty of transcendent justice and compassion. If we lose contact with nature, we lose touch with much of the joy of life and with an important part of our human calling. In either case the human personality is incomplete, and human life is impoverished.

To make a human right of access to nature real, one element is this recognition that human alienation from natural life is a significant personal, social, and ecological problem.

Churches could explore the psychological, spiritual, and moral dimensions of this problem. If we did so, we would be drawn closer to the environmental movement that is already anxious about the social and ecological dimensions of this alienation.

Another element can be educating Americans to be aware of our right of access to nature. The schools could begin such education. Each boy and girl should grow up knowing animals and plants. Each should have training and experience in tending and caring for some life. Children should be exposed, as well, to wild landscapes and ecosystems that sustain themselves, where the human roles are to tread softly, to learn from other life forms, to experience the beauty and to protect life.

A third element is to develop social facilities that support access to nature. Urbanism does not itself prevent good access. Indeed, if this planet is to support a large human population and flourishing natural life as well, many humans may need to live in compact settlements. Access to nature for urban people requires good city parks, public transportation to rural areas, affordable vacation housing, and a diversity of ways to engage with natural life systems, including public arts and conservation programs. Rural communities need to be prepared to receive urban visitors, to allow access to rural lands, to protect scenic and aesthetic features, and to enhance the diversity of rural ecosystems.

Rather than continue with illustrations of how we might develop a human right of access to nature, I want to focus on a particular example, which is my second proposal: reopening the frontier.

Access to Land: Reopening the Frontier

The frontier as we remember it was an experiment in democracy developed under the leadership of Thomas Jefferson. When Jefferson drafted the Declaration of Independence he replaced the affirmation of "life, liberty, and property," which the first Continental Congress had endorsed two years before, with the more sonorous affirmation of "Life, Liberty and the pursuit of Happiness."[23] This was fortunate. There were some who wanted to assert a right to property simply to protect their own large estates from the claims of the landless.

Jefferson did affirm a right to property, but the right he believed in was a universal right of access to land. He despised the European pattern of aristocratic estates worked by landless serfs. He believed that in America the right to property could be cast in a new way. In 1775 he wrote that "the political institutions of America, its various soils and climates opening certain resources to the unfortunate and to the enterprising of every country (ensure) to them the acquisition and possession of property."[24] A year later, in 1776, the Virginia Bill of Rights affirmed that one generation could not hold property in a manner that prevented members of the next generation from acquiring land as well.

> All men are by nature equally free and independent, and have certain inherent rights, of which, when they enter into a state of society, they cannot by any compact deprive or divest their posterity; namely, the enjoyment of life and liberty, with the means of acquiring and possessing property, and pursuing happiness and safety.[25]

Beneath his agrarian sentimentality Jefferson had a tough political insight. He did say, "No occupation is so delightful to me as the culture of the earth."[26] He rhapsodized that "those who labor in the earth are the chosen people of God, if ever He had a chosen people, whose breasts He has made His peculiar deposit for substantial and genuine virtue."[27] This enthusiasm was a front for a political strategy. Democracy was Jefferson's highest value. Democracy required persons capable of self-government. To learn self-government, a person should have a measure of both independence and security. The best means to achieve this was to own a homestead from which one could obtain subsistence. Small farmers could be free from subservience to human masters by "looking up to heaven, (and) to their own soil and industry."[28] If the backbone of the body politic was formed by such independent men and women, free institutions would be preserved.

Jefferson believed that for democracy to endure, it was essential that any family be able to secure a homestead it could own outright. He believed the "right to labour the earth" was "fundamental" and that "a right to property is founded in our natural wants, in the means with which we were endowed to satisfy those wants, and the right to what we acquire by those means without violating the similar rights of other sensible beings."[29] Jefferson implemented his political strategy by helping to enact laws for homesteading, first in Virginia, then in the Ohio territory, and later by negotiating the Louisiana Purchase, which secured for the United States lands that seemed endless. A free people would remain independent, hardworking, and creative, because each family would have access to land for their own use.

Similar motivation lay behind the jubilee laws in the biblical Sabbath tradition. People needed access to land if they were to retain the freedom that they won when the Lord led them into the Promised Land.

Since the risks of agriculture are great, and not all are equally successful, land tends to aggregate into the hands of fewer and fewer people. So there need to be occasions for redistribution, for starting over. I believe that any civilized society needs an orderly system for the periodic redistribution of land. The alternative is the growing oppression of the landless, which leads toward slavery and revolution.

We have been taught to regard land as wealth. Some have called it the only true wealth. But land is not wealth in the same sense as buildings and equipment or stocks and bonds. The ownership of land is always conditioned by a social interest: land is too important to society for it to be appropriated absolutely by the individual. The Bible affirms that God also retains a prior claim to land: "No land shall be sold outright, because the land is mine, and you are coming into it as aliens and settlers. . . . You shall allow land which has been sold to be redeemed."[30] And I will suggest shortly that the land has rights of its own that society must recognize.

The human relation to land mixes property relations with personal relations. We may draw livelihood from land, and land has tangible value in society: these are characteristics of wealth. But land is also vital and alive, reaching out to me in special ways. Land engages my sensory, emotional, and aesthetic capacities. It lays claims on me while I claim it. So relating to land is something like a marriage: the relationship thrives if I take delight and acknowledge mutual responsibilities.

Jefferson's systems served as well for a century, making America the land of opportunity for Western civilization, establishing the most free and creative society in human history. But the land finally ran out, and after a while the process of consolidation began. In 1920 there were 32 million Americans on farms, 30 percent of our population. By 1980 only about 6 million, 3 percent of our population lived on farms. [31] Of those remaining on the farm, most have abandoned subsistence: they buy Wonderbread and canned vegetables at the supermarket; they mortgage their farms to the hilt; they are just as immersed in the cash economy as the manufacturer or the factory worker.

Today the slums of our cities teem with millions for whom there is no work, and never will be, from one generation to another. Even though conservative capitalists are in office—perhaps because they are in office—the Western world's cash economy is beginning to unravel again, as it did before previous worldwide depressions. Job opportunities are shrinking and wages are beginning to fall; commodity and mineral prices are declining; debts that can never be repaid are piling up at home and abroad. As the screws tighten, we will be pushed to exploit each other and to exploit land and environment ever more harshly. It is a wicked predicament for a once free people.

Part of the answer is to reopen the frontier, to make land available again to any landless family who desires it and is willing to live there and invest themselves in the land.

The first step is to legislate that the holding of lands by profit-seeking corporations is inherently inappropriate. Land requires tending—a mutual and moral relationship. By their very character, corporations can function only to secure profit: their bottom-line nature forces them to regard land as a commodity and to exploit it.

A next step would be to establish regional land courts that would inventory corporate lands and private holdings exceeding a size set by law. As demand for homesteads developed, these courts would "draft," by lottery, lands of the appropriate character, set their value, purchase them by condemnation, divide them into small functional units, and distribute them with conditional leases to homesteaders, who, if they live on the land and improve it, may secure clear title after five years. Those preparing to homestead should receive training in the care of land, followed by supervision during the time of their leasehold.

I would not limit homesteading to the poor, just to those who do not already own real estate. I would not limit it to agricultural lands. This is not just a scheme to perpetuate small farms. I believe, with Jefferson, that the right of access to land is fundamental to human freedom. Each person or family should be able to exercise that right once in a lifetime, regardless of how they propose to use the land. Some would want to farm. Probably more people would want to have a place of their own but earn a salary away from the land. Most people would likely not choose to homestead, because the hard work and personal risks would be intimidating. But the right to a homestead would be there for anyone who decided to start over. The land court could sort the lands it condemned to fit the needs of different homesteaders. Prime farmland, for example, should be reserved for promising farmers.

I would expect that at first only a few would exercise their right to homestead: some migrant farmworkers, some children of farmers, some young adventurers, some in mid-life crisis, some at retirement, a few of those laid off from heavy industry, a few from the perpetually unemployed in urban slums, some people with strong religious and environmental ideals. But the existence of a homesteading right would stimulate individuals and institutions in our society to recover the arts of living on the land and to improve them—arts that once flourished in America but are now nearly lost. The right to a homestead might rekindle that sense of freedom and independence, those creative dreams and energies that once built America.

After a decade or two, I would expect a large migration from the cities that would rebuild rural America. Additionally, some of this new learning about homesteading and small farming would be more relevant to the needs of the Third World than the technologies of corporate agriculture that we now export.

It will take a while to win back this fundamental American right to a homestead that Jefferson helped establish for our first century. Meanwhile, we can begin to learn the arts and improve the sciences that comprise a rural culture where people can support themselves and land can be cared for. Giant agribusiness and its subsidiaries—including the United States Department of Agriculture and the land-grant universities—are more likely to hinder than help this effort. We will have to look to more flexible and humane institutions, including churches.

Thank God there is at least one church that has preserved an agricultural vision in America. We have regarded the Amish as a curiosity, but they may turn out to be one of our most important cultural and agricultural resources. The Amish are not perfect; they provide us with a witness but not a blueprint. They witness to the fact that it is still possible in America to farm while improving, not depleting, the land. They witness that it is possible to select among technologies on moral grounds and still farm efficiently and profitably.

The Amish also witness to the fact that farming is part of a productive, rural-community culture, not just an individual endeavor. Farming is more a culture than a business. Responsible agriculture requires complex cooperation among farmers and with smiths, mechanics, teachers, traders, researchers, and many others. Though some of this cooperation may be hired, agriculture requires a community where there is a complex of barter and exchange at the local level. Community relationships must be deeper and more dependable than the availability of cash payment. The intimate economics of community survival and a willingness to pull each other through hard times must be valued more than the distant, impersonal market. When agriculture is transformed into agribusiness, it begins to decline, however impressive its exploitive efficiencies may seem in the short run.

Responsible agriculture requires constant attention to basic moral values. Agriculture needs a church—or something similar to a church—that is central to the lives of its people. To prepare the way for reopening the frontier, I believe we should experiment with intentional Christian communities of small farmers, along with others who have supporting skills. We have a lot to learn about how people and land may support each other again.

CONSTITUTIONAL RIGHTS FOR NATURE

To balance human manipulation of nature, I propose the right of nature to protection and standing within our constitutional system. It is time to extend constitutional rights to life to all species that God created and delights in, and rights also to the critical ecological systems of clean air, pure water, soils, and terrain that sustain life.

The needs of all life should be represented in the decisions that affect life. We can see the truth of this at the practical level, such as a farm. If a farm is plowed and planted for maximum immediate yield without thought for its productive future, the soil will weaken and erode, and both farm and farmer may be impoverished as years pass. Farming must depend on biological processes that convert the energy of the sun into foods that ultimately nourish humans. A good farmer is sensitive to the character of the environment within which he or she farms: climate, terrain, water cycles, soil structure, biological capabilities. The best farming increases the biological life and productive capability of the land.

We also see that we must protect the earth's life systems at the planetary level. Human life depends upon them. The earth's systems of life and energy are flexible and responsive. They can be enriched by human culture, but they can also be damaged by human abuse. Since human technologies now have impact upon so much of the earth, we can no longer ignore our ecological influence. We cannot destroy the ozone layer and expect to avoid cancer, nor can we deplete the earth's forest cover and expect to breathe oxygen. Human survival now requires sophisticated knowledge of the earth's ecosystems and a willingness to accommodate to their characteristics.

As we translate these insights into laws and social policies, our efforts are impeded by the humanocentric perspective built into our constitutional system. Today public environmental decisions must be justified by their influence on human welfare. For example, we have laws that require "environmental impact statements" prior to major federal land-use decisions. But what is actually assessed under these laws is the impact of the environmental change on *human* welfare. Showing that a significant environment will be damaged is not enough to halt a dam or a power plant. One must show that the ultimate injury to human welfare will be greater than the anticipated benefit of the project. The needs of environment itself are not directly represented in this decision-making process.

It is true that by law we protect endangered species. We justify this anomaly by arguing that species diversity is in the long-term interest of human welfare.

In the Bible, Sabbath law required that the land be left fallow from time to time and that wild animals have access to it. The reason was not that humans would ultimately benefit, though they might. The reason was that the land was the Lord's. God had regard for it and gave it, as well as people, a right to rest. Likewise, wild animals were part of the Lord's creation and called upon God for food. God heard their prayers. God was concerned that they have access to food. Though the social implications of the Lord's relation to nature are not fully developed in the Bible, there is a recognition that every vital aspect of creation has value to the Lord. God expects humans to respect all types of life, not because they are useful, but because they are God's creatures.

The United States Constitution applies not only to some 240 million people, but also to 3,600,000 square miles of land

and perhaps one million additional square miles of coastal and territorial waters. These lands and waters teem with complex systems of life. The trees and soil, the rivers, lakes, and estuaries, the populations of birds, fish, and mammals have a right to life also—not an absolute right, but a right that must be considered in relation to human rights. The systematic interrelations of earth, air, water, and living organisms must be taken into account in decisions that affect them. Impairing these interrelations so that damage spreads through a significant ecosystem should not be permitted.

The first public figure to suggest how our legal system might be adapted to this need was Supreme Court Justice William O. Douglas. In addition to being the Court's leading defender of human rights, Douglas was a leader in environmental protection. In 1972 he wrote a dissenting opinion in support of the Sierra Club's claim to represent the undeveloped Mineral King Valley in California against Walt Disney Enterprises' wish to build a ski resort. The question was whether anyone had the legal right to speak for a natural environment.

Douglas proposed enlarging the community of those who could seek protection under our legal system. To this end he cited Aldo Leopold's observation that a "land ethic simply enlarges the boundaries of the community to include soils, waters, plants and animals, or collectively, the land."[32] Douglas argued that "contemporary public concern for protecting nature's ecological equilibrium should lead to the conferral of standing upon environmental objects to sue for their own preservation."[33]

Douglas noted that we have already given such legal standing to several entities that are not persons. Under common law ships have legal rights to sue or be sued, independent of their owner or captain. Corporations, which are creations of the state, are treated as persons under the law and have been given many of the constitutional protections that persons enjoy. They have standing in court, and the law allows persons to speak for them as it allows persons to speak for children and the mentally incompetent. "So it should be," Douglas argued:

. . . as respects valleys, alpine meadows, rivers, lakes, estuaries, beaches, ridges, groves of trees, swampland, or even
air that feels the destructive pressures of modern technology
and modern life. The river, for example, is the living symbol
of all the life it sustains or nourishes—fish, aquatic insects,
water ouzels, otter, fisher deer, elk, bear, and all other
animals, including man, who are dependent on it or who enjoy it for its sight, its sound, or its life. The river as plaintiff
speaks for the ecological unit of life that is part of it. Those
people who have a meaningful relation to that body of
water—whether it be a fisherman, a canoeist, a zoologist, or
a logger—must be able to speak for the values which the river
represents and which are threatened with destruction. . . .

I do not know Mineral King. . . . Those who hike it, fish
it, hunt it, camp in it, or frequent it, or visit it merely to sit
in solitude and wonderment are legitimate spokesmen for it,
whether they be few or many. . . . Those people who have
so frequented the place as to know its values and wonders will
be able to speak for the entire ecological community. [34]

Douglas's proposal has not attracted support within the
Supreme Court. We are not likely to extend rights to nature
until there is public understanding of why this is appropriate.

Through two centuries of American constitutional history
we have extended political rights to new groups and broad-
ened the application of rights already stated. In our generation we have deepened our understanding of the rights of
blacks, the rights of women, the rights of children, the rights
of the unborn. Let us now bring the rights of nature into this
discussion of basic constitutional values.

I believe that proposing a constitutional amendment may
be the most effective way to place this issue on the national
agenda. Like ending slavery or giving women the vote, extending civil rights to nature will probably require such a
basic change. Here, to start discussion, is my draft for an
amendment:

All life shall be treated with considerateness, since the earth
is vulnerable to human activity. While human harvest of life
and resources and physical expressions of human society are
appropriate, it shall be a constitutional responsibility to pro-

tect species of life, singular natural features, and the functioning of major life systems. Species, systems of life support, and natural features shall have legal standing to protect their interests within the general welfare.

It is my intention that this language not inhibit harvest of animals or plants that are not threatened species. The only right conferred upon individuals within species is the right to considerate treatment. "Considerateness" means having regard for the needs or feelings of others. The ethics of considerateness will evolve as our understanding and appreciation of other species deepens. At the least, this language would strengthen the legal prohibition against cruelty to animals.

The physical development of human society—the extension of our roads; the construction of new buildings, airports, dams, and facilities; the conversion of land to agriculture and other human use—would have to adapt to the need to protect species of life, singular natural features, and the functioning of major life systems. Competing claims would be resolved by appeal to "the general welfare," which is a developed concept in our legal system. But *now* general welfare would include environmental health as well as human welfare.

Of the three environmental interests I propose for constitutional protection, "species of life" is the most specific and unambiguous. We know how to distinguish species. Human efforts to protect them are becoming sophisticated. There may still be noxious species, such as the Mediterranean fruit fly, which we prefer to remove from most environments in the interest of general welfare. But this amendment would require us to assure that viable populations of such species are retained in special areas.

"Major life systems" is a less specific interest intended to include not only living things, but the natural materials and forces that support life. These may be the patterns of air and water movement on a continental or worldwide scale, or the specific characteristics of materials and forces within a major ecosystem. Although these ecological relationships are real, the demarcation of ecosystems involves arbitrary human definition of boundaries. Guidelines for definition would need to be established by law.

"Singular natural features" is the most subjective of the environmental interests I propose to protect. It does not relate to the survival of life so much as to the quality of life. It relates not just to characteristics within natural phenomena, but to the aesthetic interaction between humanity and nature. This aesthetic interaction has led our society to decide, for example, that the Grand Canyon is more appropriate for a park than for a hydroelectric dam site. Much of the environmental protection achieved during the past century—including national parks, wild and scenic rivers, and national monuments—expresses this desire to protect singular natural features. This amendment would strengthen the hand of those seeking to protect distinctive areas from human alteration. It, too, would require legislative definition of criteria. The amendment would stimulate us to ponder what it is, in addition to life support, that we value in the natural world around us.

In addition to giving rights to three types of environmental interest, the amendment would place upon American citizens and governments a "constitutional responsibility to protect. . . ." Though in moral discussion we recognize that people have responsibilities as well as rights, specifying a responsibility within the American constitution would be a novelty. It is appropriate in this instance because the natural life and interests that this amendment protects are inarticulate and must depend upon human initiatives to obtain their rights. Some persons or organizations who become aware of threats to natural life would need to use the amendment to persuade or require government to enforce the rights that the amendment recognizes.

PEACE WITH LAND

In conclusion, I take note of the human religious impulse to see divinity in nature or through nature. Biblical religions resist this impulse. We affirm that people know God primarily through God's direct words to us, which culminate in the

"Word made flesh," Jesus Christ. There is also another human impulse that treats nature as a thing: conquering it, manipulating it, doing with nature whatever we want. I believe that biblical revelation also rejected this impulse. Jesus reminded us that God clothes the grass of the field with beauty King Solomon could not equal. [35] God has regard for all creation, not just for us.

We are called neither to worship nor to abuse nature, but to live creatively and productively together with our fellow creatures. This exhibits the image of God in us: to tend and keep the earth as God would have it kept.

For modern Americans to do this, we must open opportunities for human beings to come in contact with natural life. We must affirm the birthright of each to have access to land. When the powerful push the weak off the land, they call it efficiency; but it is really oppression. It is violence. It feeds the war machine. The prophet Micah understood that the road to peace includes giving people their land back. He promised that God intends to do just that.

> They will hammer their swords into ploughshares, and their spears into sickles. . . . There will be no more training for war. Each person will sit under their vine and their fig tree with no one to trouble them. The mouth of the Yahweh Sabaoth has spoken it. [36]

Today we need moral training and appropriate technology, so that when we homestead, we will not ape the oppression of corporate farming nor fall back to the desperate, hard-scrabble tenancy of our ancestors, but rather engage nature productively in respect, love, and creativity.

Peace on earth includes sustainable ecological peace, peace among the species, and peace with our natural environment. Humans need to learn that we share the earth with others who have value in God's eyes and who justly claim our consideration and our protection. Rights extend to all life. All creatures wait for Christians to set them free from slavery. All creatures look forward to praising the Savior who has made them free indeed. When John on Patmos looked toward the fulfillment of history, he heard "all living things in creation—everything that lives in the air, and on the ground, and under the ground, and in the sea, crying, 'To the One who is sitting on the throne and to the Lamb, be all praise, honor, glory and power, for ever and ever.'"[37]

1. Gal 5:1, Jerusalem Bible Version (hereafter JBV).

2. Rom 8:19, 21, JBV.

3. Exod 23:10-12, New English Bible (hereafter NEB).

4. Exod 21:2, Revised Standard Version (hereafter RSV).

5. Lev 19:9, 10, NEB.

6. Gen 1:12; 1:20-22, NEB.

7. Lev 19:2, King James Version.

8. Lev 25:4, 5, NEB.

9. Lev 26:33-35, NEB.

10. Lev 25:23, NEB.

11. Lev 25:13, NEB.

12. Prov 22:28, RSV.

13. Neh 5:1-13, RSV.

14. Amos 8:4-8, NEB.

15. Job 31:38-40, NEB.

16. Lev 21:22, RSV.

17. Ps 85:10-12, NEB.

18. Walter Brueggemann, *The Land* (Philadelphia: Fortress Press, 1977), p. 157. This thesis that invading tribes stimulated peasant revolts was initially developed in a brilliant article by George Mendenhall, "The Hebrew Conquest of Palestine," *Biblical Archaeologist*, No. 25 (1962), pp. 66–87; reprinted in *Biblical Archaeologist Reader* 3 (Garden City, N.Y.: Doubleday, 1970), pp. 100–120.

19. Lev 26:3, 4, 13, RSV.

20. John Muir, from *John of Mountains*, quoted in Michael P. Cohen, *The Pathless Way: John Muir and American Wilderness* (Madison: University of Wisconsin Press, 1984) p. 196.

21. *Ibid.*, p. 130.

22. Rom 8:19-21, JBV.

23. Declaration and Resolves of the First Continental Congress, October 14, 1774; and the Declaration of Independence, July 4, 1776; in Henry Steele Commager, ed., *Documents of American History* (New York: Appleton-Century-Crofts, 1949), pp. 83–101.

24. Jefferson's draft of the Declaration on Taking up Arms, July 6, 1775, as quoted by A. Whitney Griswold, "The Agrarian Democracy of Thomas Jefferson," *The American Political Science Review*, Vol. 40, no. 4 (August 1946) p. 674.

25. Commager, ed., *Documents of American History, op. cit.*, p. 103.

26. Jefferson, quoted in Griswold, *op. cit.*, p. 662.

27. Thomas Jefferson, "Notes on the State of Virginia," in Adrienne Koch & William Paden, *The Life and Selected Writings of Thomas Jefferson* (New York: Modern Library, 1972), p. 280.

28. Jefferson, quoted in Griswold, *op. cit.*, p. 672.

29. Jefferson, quoted in Griswold, *op. cit.*, p. 672.

30. Lev 25:23, 24, NEB.

31. *A Time to Choose: Summary Report on the Structure of Agriculture* (Washington, D.C.: U.S. Department of Agriculture, 1981), p. 34.

32. Aldo Leopold, *A Sand County Almanac* (New York and San Francisco: Sierra Club/Ballantine, 1966), p. 239.

33. William O. Douglas's dissent in *Sierra Club v. Morton*, as reprinted in Christopher D. Stone, *Should Trees Have Standing? Toward Legal Rights for Natural Objects* (Los Altos, Calif.: William Kaufmann, Inc., 1974), p. 239. In his opinion Douglas referred to the writing of Christopher Stone where this idea is developed more fully.

34. *Ibid.*, pp. 74, 83.

35. Matt 6:28-30; Luke 12:27, 28.

36. Mic 4:3, 4, JBV, altered.

37. Rev 5:13, JBV.

The Virgil Michel Chair seeks to promote a greater understanding of the cultural and social questions faced by rural America; to promote an intelligent awareness of these issues in the Church; and to formulate ways of mobilizing the resources of churches and their ministers in promoting the quality of rural life. The current occupant of the chair, Dr. Bernard Evans, directs the Rural Ministry Program in the School of Theology at St. John's University, Collegeville, Minnesota.

NATIONAL CATHOLIC RURAL LIFE CONFERENCE

The National Catholic Rural Life Conference aims to bring the perspectives of Scripture and Catholic tradition to current problems and issues confronting rural people and communities in the United States. The conference serves as a national support office for diocesan rural life directors. Issues receiving conference attention at this time include the rural crisis, food and agriculture, and land ethics.